# Toilets, Bricks, Fish Hooks and Pride

## THE PEAK PERFORMANCE TOOLBOX _EXPOSED_

*This book is being given to*

---

*because I care about you and your success*

---

## BRIAN M. CAIN, MS, CMAA

Brian Cain Peak Performance, LLC

## What Champions Are Saying About Brian Cain

"Brian, thank you for everything you have given to the success of our program. You're truly a Master of the Mental Game. Understanding that when you have done everything within your control to prepare, you should remove the outcome from the equation and focus entirely on the process. In doing so, you give yourself the best chance for success which truly unlocks your potential to accomplish great things. When you play in the moment, pitch to pitch for the entire game, and you can look back and are satisfied with your effort, that is giving yourself the best chance for success, and that is all anyone can ask. Thanks for everything you have given to Tomball baseball."

### *Rick Lynch, High School Coach*

"I was introduced to Brian Cain at a Coaches Clinic in Houston, Texas. Over the past 25 years, I have heard numerous clinicians and speakers and Brian compares with the best. He is exceptional. He is entertaining, informative and a very passionate speaker. I found myself time and time again thinking, this guy is awesome. His use of video footage and computer graphics was exceptional. He spoke on the mental game, team chemistry and goal setting. I would recommend Brian to anyone who wants their team or program to reach the next level."

### *Mark Thigpen, High School Coach*

"Brian is a dynamic speaker and teacher when it comes to the mental game of baseball. He has great stories, presentations and practices that not only promote individual mental toughness, but also team toughness. He teaches you how to deal with the constant adversity that arises in the game and in life. I use some of his techniques not only with my pitchers but in my everyday life."

"Cain is the world's #1 Peak Performance Coach for mixed martial arts fighters. Preparation for competition is typically 90% physical and 10% mental, yet competitions are often 90% mental and 10% physical. Cain gives you strategies and systems to work at your mental game better than anyone I have ever heard before. If you are a serious athlete, you need to try his PRIDE program."

*Rob "Maximus" MacDonald,*
*Mixed Martial Arts Fighter*
*Professional Strength and Conditioning Coach*

"Brian Cain brings an enthusiasm and strength of character that are contagious. He is "into" everything he does, from communicating with athletic directors, coaches, parents and athletes about success, to motivating groups anxious to lend an ear. He enters each situation with a passion and honesty which is both refreshing as well as motivating. He engages people, and respectfully challenges them to make their dreams become a reality. Brian is one of those special people who always make you feel better after you talk with him. I would encourage everyone to make the contact. You will be a better person for the effort."

*Dan Marlow, CMAA, High School Athletic Director*

"Cain's ability to teach the Mental Game to players and coaches at any level is outstanding. His ideas and strategies for implementing change are unique and effective. I got more out of his class than any workshop or clinic I have attended in the last 20 years. If you want to provide a learning experience for your coaches and athletes that will change their lives, you need to expose them to Brian Cain. It will be the best investment you ever make for your athletic department."

*Michael O'Day, CMAA, High School Athletic Director*
*2005 NIAAA National Citation Award Winner*
*2005 VSADA Athletic Director of The Year*

# Toilets, Bricks, Fish Hooks and PRIDE

UPDATED THIRD EDITION

## THE PEAK PERFORMANCE TOOLBOX *EXPOSED*

**BRIAN M. CAIN, MS, CMAA**

Brian Cain Peak Performance, LLC

www.BrianCain.com
www.BrianCainInnerCircle.com
www.ToiletsBricksFishHooksAndPride.com
www.SoWhatNextPitch.com
www.MentalConditioningManual.com

Peak Performance Publishing

Brian M. Cain, MS, CMAA
Peak Performance Coach
Peak Performance Publishing
Brian Cain Peak Performance, LLC

Toilets, Bricks, Fish Hooks and Pride: The Peak Performance
Toolbox Exposed
A Masters of the Mental Game Series Book

Printed in the USA
Edited by: Jim LeVine, Ph.D., Jackson Penfield-Cyr and Justin
Dedman
Cover design and book layout: Doris Bruey and Daniel Yeager
Illustrations: Nicole Ludwig and Greg Pajala
Photography: Don Whipple and Matt Brown


Brian M. Cain, MS, CMAA
Toilets, Bricks, Fish Hooks and PRIDE:
The Peak Performance Toolbox Exposed
A Masters of the Mental Game Series Book
3rd Edition

Library of Congress Control Number: 2010937654
ISBN: 978-1492261322

# PREFACE

The intent of the author in writing this book in the Masters of the Mental Game Series was that it would be read one chapter at a time. The success stories featured in this book each contain information unique to the coach, athlete or program being highlighted, yet the fundamental principles of performance remain the same throughout.

This is a book for people looking for simple yet effective ways to improve their performance. This book is about what has worked for real people in real programs and not a book designed to discuss theory or read like a text book. Whether you are a veteran of the mental game or a rookie just getting started, *Toilets, Bricks, Fish Hooks and PRIDE* will give you insight and information you can use to help unlock your potential and perform at your best when it means the most.

The title of this book contains four key visualization concepts the author used to inspire mental game mastery: **Toilets** flush away the negative thinking, adversity and failure that are inherent in sport; mental **bricks** symbolize the weight that we carry when we are not able to use our toilet to flush away the negativity; **fish hooks** are symbolic of staying in the moment, focused on what you can control and what you are trying to accomplish vs. getting caught up or "hooked" on the things you can't control and are trying to avoid; and **PRIDE** is an acronym for the goal of this book, to help performers take PERSONAL RESPONSIBILITY IN DAILY EXCELLENCE which leads to being more prepared, more confident and more successful.

Here is to your competing one pitch, one shot, one shift, one down, one possession, one point, one touch, one dive, and one exchange at a time and to your enjoyment of the journey through *Toilets, Bricks, Fish Hooks and PRIDE* one chapter at a time.

Visit www.ToiletsBricksFishHooksAndPride.com
For FREE Extras, Updates & Information

# DEDICATION

This book is dedicated to the wonderful people I have met serving as a Peak Performance Coach and Athletic Director; to the people who shared their time, energy and talents that make up the principle content of this book; to my high school football coach John T. Allen for giving me a model to follow; to my mentor Dr. Ken Ravizza, whom I thank for taking me under his wing and showing me the fundamentals of the Mental Game; and to my mother, Carol Ann Cain, who lost her battle with Lung Cancer on August 2, 2010. Mom, you were not able to read this book, but provided me with a model of mental toughness to follow from day one. You are the most mentally tough person I have ever known.

# ACKNOWLEDGEMENTS

It is with sincere and deep appreciation that I acknowledge the support and guidance of the following people who helped make this book possible.

Special thanks to Bruce Brown, Pat Williams, Dr. Rob Gilbert, Ed Agresta, Harvey Dorfman, Lou Pavlovich, Jr. Dr. Ken Ravizza, Patrick Murphy, Mike Bianco, Tim Corbin, Dave Serrano, George Horton, Peter Moscariello, Ron Eastman, Rick Lynch, Mike Coutts, Jim Schlossnagle, and and the thousands of other coaches and athletes that have shared their stories and have helped influence the writing of this book.

I also give a high five for the coaching staffs, administration and student athletes of North Country Union High School and Mt. Mansfield Union High School for supporting me in my journey.

And finally, I give a GET BIG thank you to Don Whipple, Matt Brown, Nicole Ludwig, Greg Pajala, Doris Bruey, Meghan Turcot, Jim Levine, and Jackson Penfield-Cyr for their artistic and editorial contributions that made this book come to life.

# CONTENTS

Visit www.ToiletsBricksFishHooksAndPride.com
For FREE Extras, Updates & Information

# FORWARD

I have experienced how vital the mental game is to athletic success. When we won the national championship in 2004, the mental game was a huge part of our approach. In fact, without it, we wouldn't have won the national championship that season. Unfortunately, we didn't place the same emphasis on the six inches between the ears during our trips to Omaha in 2001 and 2003.

Confidence, preparation, focus on the present moment, having a positive attitude and choosing to evaluate success on the process as well as the outcome are all mental skills that can be developed just like the physical skills that need to be developed to excel in sports. Teaching the people you coach the importance of being in the moment, in the single practice, and in the now, fully focused on doing what's in front of them, is an aspect of coaching we all can too easily overlook. I've learned the hard way that success in any sport is really the sum of all of our todays.

Working on what you can control, for example, your own performance, instead of what you can't control, for example other teams' performance are such simple determinations in mastering the mental game that we often overlook them. Similarly, the things that are most elementary are often the hardest things to do on a consistent basis. Staying positive by embracing adversity and focusing on what we want instead of what we are trying to avoid can be a challenge because so much in sport is about damage control and embracing adversity instead of running away from it.

Early in my career I fell into the trap of seeing adversity as the enemy. I now realize that teams don't need every call to go their way to win. Besides, they can't control everything that happens -- the bad bounce, the freak injury, or the bad call by an umpire. All we really can control is our response to those events – *response, not reaction*. Choosing our own response is another fundamental of mental toughness.

In this book, Brian Cain has shared the fundamentals of sports psychology and peak performance that will help you to win. The valuable advice contained in these pages are many of the principles we used to help our team go from 15-16 at the midpoint of the season to winning a national championship. Brian has learned from the best of the best in Dr. Ken Ravizza and has continued to surround himself with top coaches, athletes and programs in the country. Captured in this book is the wisdom he has acquired from working with these coaches and athletes -- putting into words what they do to help perform at their best when it means the most.

I think you will find this book easy to read, fundamental and applicable to any coach or athlete looking to take their performance to another level. The people featured in this book share similar aspects of the mental game that have helped them to be successful. As Cain would say, the fundamentals are the fundamentals. They are simple to understand, but are never easy to master.

*George Horton, Head Baseball Coach,*
*1997-2007 - California State University, Fullerton*
*2004 NCAA National Champions*
*2004 ABCA National Coach of the Year*
*2008-Present - The University of Oregon*

# INTRODUCTION

Many people ask me to name the single most important factor that determines success in any and all sports activity beyond natural athletic talent; to them, I answer, "mental toughness." This is the ability to handle adversity in its many forms including mishaps, errors of judgment, weakness, untimely coincidence, injury, pressure, unexpected strategies, cheating, psychological tactics, and hostility.

A mentally tough athlete embraces adversity by recognizing that adversity, rapidly considering countermeasures, and taking effective and timely action. When we, as coaches, see this kind of mental toughness displayed in an athlete, we know we've got a winner on our team. Most of us would be overwhelmed if all of our team members possessed this kind of power. Why? Because I think we all know deep down that a mentally tough athlete can be a game changer on the playing field and a producer of significant advantages against any and all opponents, including naturally gifted athletes. Hard work beats talent when talent does not work hard.

What is mental toughness? Is it a character trait? Is it bravery, courage, belief, self-esteem, confidence, competitiveness, will power, stubbornness or motivation? Is it inate drive, attitude, good parental training or genetic hardwiring? I think it's some of all of that, probably resident in different proportions in everyone; however, I think the majority of mental toughness is taught by great coaches and can be learned just like any other skill.

Do athletes come equipped with mental toughness to their sports teams? In my experience, some do and some don't. All have the ability to develop the skill. I believe that mental toughness can be successfully developed in athletes by coaches who: 1) develop their own knowledge and system for training skills in mental toughness; 2) get to know and assess their athletes' potential thoroughly and accurately; and 3) apply their new knowledge in setting up and operating effective mental toughness development systems in their athletic programs.

As a coach, when an athlete is accepted into your program without the mental toughness skills necessary to succeed, you as the coach are taking on a significant responsibility. This athlete will become your legacy upon which your reputation will be built. If this athlete leaves your program without mental toughness and then does something because of it that manifests in a negative outcome, this outcome will reflect on you, be attributable to you and belong to you despite all of the others – parents, teachers, coaches, who may have contributed to this outcome who came before you. If athletes come in to your program without mental toughness that is their fault, but if they leave your program without mental toughness, that is YOUR fault.

The majority of the coaches and athletes reading this book will probably not earn a living in professional sport. The numbers tell the truth, and very few coaches and athletes make it to the highest level. To get there, you have to be very abnormal. Very few, if any of the athletes will ever come back into the coach's office and say, "Thanks for teaching me how to throw a curveball coach. It has made all the difference in my life." However, many athletes will come back and thank their coaches for teaching them how to be honest, respectable, and mentally tough people that have taken to heart the skills that they have been taught and used those skills to become successful in life.

Seeing the huge returns coaches get back by contributing to the long-term prosperity of these athletic participants is what has motivated me to make my life's mission the teaching of the fundamental skills of peak performance. The mental toughness that athletes carry with them into all aspects of their lives is a lasting legacy that is made accessible through the skills they can learn through participation in athletics, if athletes have a coach that teaches mental toughness. Sport by itself will not teach you anything. Coaches are the teachers, not the sport itself.

While all of what is contained in this book, described to you by coaches, have helped many athletic participants to win games, hoist more trophies and hang more banners; ultimately the fundamentals here are the foundations of success that you will see on display in any sport, or any profession outside of athletics.

The mental skills presented here are intended to provide some insight into how people have been able to train the six inches between their ears to control the six feet below it. In the broader view, these are really life skills that if they aren't learned in athletics, may never be learned. Athletics have a curious way of accessing what few other human activities do. Perhaps it's the aspect of playing a game that isn't to be taken too seriously that presents such insightful opportunity to practice at life when the stakes are lower that make it so invaluable. In such a setting, coaches stand at the ready to witness and reflect upon character building lessons that present themselves to the few souls who are ready to absorb them in such circumstances.

In this book you get inside access to some of the best coaches in the country who have taken advantage of what the mental game can offer. These coaches will be sharing with you teaching strategies and techniques that have worked for them and that will work for you when put into action.

Enjoy your journey to becoming a Master of the Mental Game. I guarantee you it will be worth your while. You should win more because of it.

Visit www.ToiletsBricksFishHooksAndPride.com
For FREE Extras, Updates & Information

# PART I

# Master The Mental Game – Terminology and Techniques

# CHAPTER 1 | MEETING THE MASTER OF THE MENTAL GAME

An Interview With Brian Cain

**Q:** Brian, you have emerged as one of the top Peak Performance Coaches in the country. Can you tell us a little about your background and how you got to where you are today?

**BC**: I was a college baseball pitcher at The University of Vermont (UVM) in the late 90s and never had the success that I thought I was capable of having. I had a good work ethic and a good attitude, but I put so much pressure on myself to succeed and be perfect, that I had no idea how to handle the adversity that comes with competing at the NCAA division one level.

I had a lot of success in high school (21-2 career record as a pitcher at Mt. Greylock Regional High School in Williamstown Massachusetts), and never really failed. So when I got to college, I kind of withdrew because I was not having success, had no idea how to handle it and was letting that frustration carry over into all aspects of my life.

I was on the borderline of having a nervous breakdown because I totally identified myself as a baseball player. When I had success I was a great guy to be around, but when I did poorly, which was the majority of the time, I was miserable, not very nice to other people, and really beat myself up much of the time.

**Q**: You were injured for the majority of your career and ended up having surgery during your junior year. At the time you thought it was the worst thing that ever happened to you because you identified so much with being a baseball player. Now looking back on it, you say that it was the best thing that ever happened to you. How did you make that shift?

**BC**: At the time of the injury and surgery during my junior year (November 1999), I was devastated. I had always been a baseball player and when that was taken away from me, I had to do some serious soul searching about my future.

My primary goal in life was to play professional ball, so when that option was gone, I decided to do the next best thing and coach college baseball. The immediate challenge before me was to figure out how to be a great coach. Now, I felt that I had always had good coaching, but there was something that was missing, preventing me from having the success I was working so hard to achieve. I suspected that if I could just discover what that missing something was, I might stand a better chance of succeeding at my new goal.

While I was in Boston on July 4th, 2000 still recovering from the elbow and shoulder surgery I had in November 1999, I went to the sports section of a Barnes & Noble bookstore to look over their baseball pitching books. I had read *The Mental Game of Baseball* by Dorfman while playing in the New England Collegiate Baseball League in the summer of 1999, and I was actually looking for one of Dorfman's other books on the mental game when I came across *Heads Up Baseball* by Ken Ravizza and Tom Hanson.

To this day I'm convinced that finding that book was probably the turning point in my life. Like a lot of college athletes, I didn't like to read, and I think at that point in my life the only book I had ever read cover-to-cover was *The Mental Game of Baseball*. Despite all of that, on that day in Barnes & Noble, I just couldn't put *Heads Up Baseball* down because I could relate so well to everything Ravizza and Hanson were describing.

**Q**: What were some of the concepts to which you could relate?

**BC**: Well, most importantly, they talked about controlling what you can control. They counseled about first being in control of yourself. They said that no one has control of what goes on around them. What can be controlled is how to respond to what goes on. That was such a simple and powerful way of looking at things that made perfect sense to me. The rest of the book was full of other great ways of managing behavior both on and off the field that once I started reading, I just couldn't put it down. The funny thing is I've had to purchase *Heads Up Baseball* three times in the past 10 years from the wear and tear I've caused marking them up and taking them everywhere I go.

One thing is for sure. This was the way I wanted to coach because I just knew it would work well for me. I also noticed that none of my coaches had ever talked about things in that way, or I had not heard them, which is perhaps why I knew deep down that the mental game was something that was missing in a lot of programs.

**Q**: You grew up in Massachusetts and played baseball at the University of Vermont. How did you ever end up doing your Master's Degree across the country at Cal State Fullerton?

**BC**: I often wonder that myself. I'm not a big believer in fate. I see that kind of rationalization as an excuse and a lack of responsibility for what happens much of the time. I prefer to believe that much of the time we are personally responsible for why things happen to our careers and our lives – the good and the not so good. I am not a believer that things happen for a reason, I believe there is a reason why things happen. Those are two totally different statements.

When I got back from Boston, I e-mailed Ken Ravizza who was a professor of sport psychology at Cal State Fullerton and told him how much I liked his book. I also mentioned that I was interested in coaching college baseball and pursuing a Master's Degree in sports psychology because I thought it would make me a much better coach. I never really expected all that much to come of it, but shortly after sending my email, I received a hand written letter from him saying that Cal State Fullerton had a graduate program in sport psychology and that he would be interested in having me come out to visit the school.

I flew from Vermont to California in November of 2000 and stayed with Ken and his graduate students for three days. I sat in on a few of his classes and presentations and met with his students. I knew immediately that this is where I needed to be and that it was the program for me. I have to be honest, I was a little scared to move across the country from Vermont to Southern California because I didn't know anyone or anything about that part of the country. But looking back, it was the best move I ever made and it has significantly changed my life for the better.

In retrospect, I can honestly say that meeting Ken and spending two years at Fullerton working with him and the Fullerton baseball staff including George Horton, Rick Vanderhook, Dave Serrano, Chad Baum and the rest of the Titans baseball program was as good a turn of events as I could have hoped for. I wish everyone could have that kind of a life-changing experience and have it related to something that is their passion and something they want to dedicate their life to.

The reason I say that the best thing that ever happened to me was getting injured during my career at Vermont was because if that never happened, I would never have picked up that book, read it, looked more closely at what was missing in my baseball and personal life and would not have had all the wonderful experiences I have had ever since because of the mental game.

I am truly grateful to Ken Ravizza, Cal State Fullerton, the Titan baseball team and all the staff at CSUF. They are the best teachers I have ever had.

**Q**: You seem to have been able to take what you learned from your time at Fullerton and share that with coaches of different sports all across the country. How is that?

**BC**: I pride myself on being a life-long learner and on learning something new and trying to get better every day, again something that comes from my Titan Baseball experience. I have been very fortunate to be able to speak at coaching clinics and work with some of the nation's top high school and collegiate programs, coaches, and athletes on developing their mental toughness. Sport psychology and peak performance coaching is a lot of fun for me because I get to meet some great people and share things that I wish I had known when I was still playing. I am fortunate that when I work with a team, I am able to learn as much from their experiences as I am able to give them insights about mental skills.

**Q**: You often talk about the differences between expensive and inexpensive experience. What are you talking about? What's the difference?

**BC**: I think everyone would agree that one of the best ways to improve is to get more experience. There are two types of experience: expensive and inexpensive. Expensive experience unfortunately is what most people get by making mistakes and from failing on their own. Unfortunately, I was stubborn and learned a lot from expensive experience. Inexpensive experience is what you get from following good advice from other people and from learning through their mistakes. I feel that I have been able to get some tremendous inexpensive experience from working with some of the best coaches and athletes across the country. I am very fortunate to have found something I love to do and to be able to make a career out of it.

Most people are hesitant to ask others for help or to pick their brain because they might look like they aren't confident or don't know something, like it is a sign of weakness to ask for help. I couldn't disagree more. If you go to an ABCA convention, where do all the great coaches sit? They sit in the front row. Why? Because they want to learn and research shows that by sitting in the front row you increase your chances of retaining information. Asking for help and for other coaches to share their experiences with you is one of the best ways to improve as a coach.

**Q**: What do you feel is the foundation of the mental game?

**BC**: For me the foundation of the mental game is what Ken Ravizza talks about in *Heads Up Baseball*. He talks about having self-control, a plan, and trusting your preparation and ability. I think he hit the nail on the head with that approach. I would also add that quality practice is probably the single most important factor in long term success. You practice a lot more than you play and improvement happens more rapidly if you increase the quality of your practice.

**Q**: You have done a lot of work on building championship team chemistry. What are some things you would encourage coaches who are looking to improve the team chemistry in their programs to try?

**BC**: I think the first thing a team needs to do is develop standards of excellence that say this is who we are and this is what we are about. I have called them team mission statements or core covenants. Coming up with standards of excellence and defining what those standards look like in school, the community, practice, and competition will provide the map a program needs to define what they are about.

In 2007, Dave Serrano, the head baseball coach at The University of California, Irvine came up with the core covenant TEAM – Toughness-Every Pitch-Anteater-Mentality. I think that signifies not only what the players are committing to but what the team needs to do to be successful in the four key areas: school, community, practice, and competition.

The best part about what Coach Serrano did at Irvine was that he got many improvement suggestions to come from the players so they would take ownership of the program and hold each other accountable. Taking this approach, a lot of the small, back stabbing problems that can go on, don't even show up because everyone has adopted the same standards of excellence and dedication to make their suggestions work.

Other things that are great for team building are activities that allow players to get to know each other and compete to accomplish a certain task. For example, if you have all your players sit in a circle with their arms around each other, and try to stand up at the same time that is a very challenging task. You need to have everyone on the same page, fully committing to the task, while listening to each other to come up with the best strategy for success.

I have come up with a *How To Develop Championship Team Chemistry* instructional DVD program and manual that can be purchased at *www.briancain.com* that takes you through developing core covenants and teaches you how to run some of the team building activities we are talking about.

**Q**: You also do phone and e-mail consulting with players and coaches from all over the world. Explain how this works.

**BC**: In this day and age of technology, it is often more convenient for people to talk on the phone or communicate through online video conferencing than it is to get together face to face. Ideally we can get together face to face, but often that is very difficult to do. What I do is work with coaches and athletes over the phone and set the groundwork and foundation of their mental game. We identify what their strengths are and where they can improve. We then come up with a plan of action to address areas of need. We stay in contact about once a week over the phone and more frequently through e-mail. If an athlete wants to take their mental game to another level, I will have them fly in and stay with me for a few days or I will go to them.

If you are interested in one-on-one coaching, they should visit www.briancain.com and send me a message from our "contact us" page and see if I have any openings left for one-on-one coaching. I cut off the number of people that I work with because I feel that getting to know the people I am working with is critical because quality work is more important than quantity. More is not always better.

**Q**: Who has been the most influential person in your career as a peak performance coach?

**BC:** Without a doubt it has been Ken Ravizza. Ken is the master of the mental game and having spent two years with him at Fullerton and maintaining a friendship with him to this day has been incredible. Many of my motivations and perspectives on life and coaching have changed completely due to my relationship with him. He is one of the most amazing people I know. If you are reading this book and have not read *Heads Up Baseball*, you need to check it out. You will see why Ken has had such a positive impact on my life.

**Q**: If you could give some advice to the coaches or players reading this book, what would it be?

**BC**: It would be that the day you stop learning is the day that you should retire. There are coaches out there that say "This is how I have been doing it for 20 years, and this is how I am going to continue to do it." As a high school athletic director, I cringe when I hear that. Just because you have been doing something for 20 years does not mean you have been doing it right for 20 years or that it is still best practice. For example, look at what has happened with static stretching. It has been replaced by a technique that was thought to be harmful for the longest time -- ballistic stretching.

Consistent and never-ending improvement is what coaching and athletics are all about today. Learning how to teach something a new way, or understanding why a dynamic warm-up is better than static stretching is critical if you want to be great year-in and year-out. I had the opportunity to work with George Horton, one of the best baseball coaches in the country, and he has a system that has proven to get results. How do I know that? Because I know there must be a reason that George takes teams to the College World Series more frequently than most. He has a system that covers every aspect of the game from the broadest to the smallest detail. Yet despite all of his knowledge, he consistently attends coaching clinics and relentlessly tries to find ways to improve his system and program.

Visit www.ToiletsBricksFishHooksAndPride.com
For FREE Extras, Updates & Information

# CHAPTER 2 | PEAK PERFORMANCE PISTOL – THE SIX GUN SHOOTER

When Everything Goes Your Way

Have you ever had one of those days where everything seemed to go your way? You did everything right and played the game of your life. Wonderful wasn't it? If you are nodding your head as you read this, you have experienced a "peak performance" moment in sport. On the other hand, when you look back on that performance, can you remember what your preparation was like or what you were thinking, or did it just kind of happen? If you can't remember, wouldn't you like to be able to recreate that performance on a consistent basis?

You've already proven that you can achieve peak performance, so there is no reason you can't get back there again. Playing at peak performance consistently can be replicated. If you did it once you can do it again. The seeds of greatness are inside of you. Understanding the six Ps of peak performance will allow you to recreate your greatest performances and will help serve as a foundation for you to consistently play at or near your best.

## PRESENT MOMENT

When athletes play at their best, it's because they are totally focused on the present moment -- the here and now. Often, this is why you can't remember what you were saying to yourself or how you were feeling during the game, because you were totally engaged in what you were doing. In short, your mind and body were one.

## THE PROCESS

When athletes play best, they focus only on the things that they can control. During peak performance, they are totally focused on the things in their circle of control – themselves and their APE (Attitude, Performance, & Effort). In contrast, when athletes focus on things that they can't control -- the weather, the other team, the officials, the politics of the team, or a slew of other things outside of their control, their performance suffers.

The process-focused athlete is not concerned with winning and losing, because outcome is out of their control. The process focused athlete is concerned with playing well and executing in the moment, because they know that winning is a byproduct of playing well and playing well is about executing in the moment.

## POSITIVE MINDSET

Most athletes are confused about having a positive mindset. They think that having a positive mindset is never getting upset about making a turnover, or losing a game. Not true. A positive mindset is focusing totally on that which you are trying to do, not what you are trying to avoid. With a positive mindset, the quarterback focuses on making a quality throw, not on trying to avoid an interception.

## PERSPECTIVE

When an athlete wins, is she fun to be around? Conversely, when she loses, is she miserable until she wins another game? If both are true, she probably has an unhealthy perspective on sport. She is most likely "personalizing the performance." When an athlete personalizes the performance, she may be putting too much pressure on herself without realizing it. She probably needs to care less about end results and focus more on enjoying the journey and the process of playing well, which will provide a healthier perspective.

**PREPARATION**

There is no more important ingredient to an athlete's success than quality preparation. Practice doesn't make perfect, practice makes permanent. It's unlikely that an athlete will perform better in games than he does in practice. If an athlete thinks as he reads this, "What is Cain talking about? I'm a gamer. I turn it on in games," then he's in trouble. If an athlete is someone who can "STEP IT UP", he will get beat every time by the person who has been practicing hard all year long and will go out there with the mindset that all he has to do is do what he's been doing all year.

If he thinks he can "STEP IT UP" in games, he needs to start stepping it up in practice. The athletes that have peak performances on a consistent basis are the athletes that don't change their intensity and focus from practice to games. They go all out in practice to make practice more game-like, so that they can make the games more practice-like.

**TAKE PRIDE**

Peak performers know that life is not like a light switch. They know that in the pursuit of excellence, they can't be less than excellent in one area of life and expect to excel in another. The light switch must always be on. Excellence is a lifestyle, not an event.

Many athletes think they can slack in school or be dishonest with their family and friends and excel on the field. Those athletes may perform well because they are more physically gifted than those who they play against, but they are NOT SUCCESSFUL. The only true measure of success is how good they are compared to how good they could be, not how good they are as compared to others.

## WIN EVERYDAY

The word WIN is an acronym for What's Important Now. If an athlete lives in the present, focuses on the process, has a positive mindset, keeps a healthy perspective on sport, increases his quality of practice, and takes pride in all that he does, regardless of what the scoreboard says, he will be a winner.

# CHAPTER 3 | WHY IS PRIDE IN THE TITLE OF THIS BOOK?

### Personally Responsible for Just 200 Feet

Brian Cain Peak Performance has produced a peak performance and mental conditioning program called PRIDE – Personal Responsibility In Daily Excellence. The program features eighteen instructional videos and a manual for the person looking to maximize their human potential.I get a lot of requests to work with high schools and colleges around the country and unfortunately I can't meet all of those requests. One of my goals has always been to create a video program that any coach, parent or athlete can use to help develop the mental skills necessary to give themselves the best chance to perform consistently at their best.

> There are no cookie cutter approaches to sport psychology or peak performance, but my experience has shown me that the best of the best, regardless of the sport or level are all utilizing some fundamental mental skills that most of the underachievers who have the potential to be excellent are not aware of. In PRIDE, I teach you many of those skills.

## WHY PRIDE?

The reason Cain called the program PRIDE is that he constantly finds himself talking about the importance of each and every day, each and every pitch and wanted to organize a system with an acronym that players and coaches could remember.

From my first day at Cal State Fullerton with Dr. Ken Ravizza and Coach George Horton, I learned the importance of TODAY and how Today + Today + Today = Your Career. I have come to realize that many coaches and athletes waste a lot of great opportunities to get better because they are too busy counting the days instead of finding ways to make the days count. With taking Personal Responsibility In Daily Excellence (PRIDE), you set daily goals that help you improve and stay focused in the grind of trying to achieve athletic excellence.

## TEACHING LIFE SKILLS

As a high school or college coach, the majority of people you coach will never make a living playing your sport, but they will make a life using the lessons you teach through athletics. Very few coaches I have ever worked with have had a player come back 10 years later and say: "Thanks for teaching me how to throw that backdoor slider. It has really made a difference in my life." However, we all know that coaches can have the greatest impact on a young person's life, sometimes greater than their other teachers and even their parents. Being called coach is a serious responsibility.

As a high school athletic director, I am constantly talking with coaches about how they teach life skills through sport. What I've found is that high school and college coaches feel that teaching life skills through sport is essential, but they often lack the time, knowledge or system to accomplish that goal. In PRIDE I feel I have put together a foundation from which coaches can teach life skills and also reap the benefits of those life skills in their teams on field performance and ultimately the scoreboard.

## THE NEXT 200FT

If you've ever attended one of Cain's VIP behind closed door sessions at a coaching conference or seminar, you have heard him make reference to The Next 200 Feet and the importance of how it relates to your athletic and life success.

If you were to drive from Burlington, Vermont to Fullerton, California and you left at midnight, and the sun decided never to come up until you arrived in California, could you still drive across the country? The answer is yes. What will help you most along your journey? Obviously a GPS will provide you with direction, but having HEADLIGHTS are what will allow you to see your path.

Headlights do not let you see from Vermont to California, but they do let you see the next 200 feet of the road. What you are to do is drive the next 200 feet over and over and over again until you get to your final destination, whatever that may be. From the high school coach looking to repeat as state champs or turn a program around, to the college coach looking to win a NCAA national championship, the task is the same. FOCUS on the next 200 feet; be relentless in your pursuit of excellence on a daily basis; stick with the process; stay positive in your approach; control what you can control, then let the results take care of themselves.

## COKE & PEPSI THEORY

Most of us think about Coke and Pepsi when we think about the soft drink industry. Yet if we were to take a blind taste test with Coke, Pepsi and a can of Sam's Cola from Wal-Mart, most of us would not be able to tell the difference. So why is it that we think about Coke and Pepsi when we think soft drinks? The reason is they advertise with clever saturation marketing and advertise about when and where to drink their beverages.

> I wanted something that people could remember. I wanted something that people could give an answer to when asked, "What do you do when you say you teach peak performance skills?" Much like Coke and Pepsi advertise so you remember their product, when coaches can advertise their beliefs with visual representation it helps athletes to remember and take ownership of those beliefs. It's not what we know as coaches that makes us smart, it's what we can train our athletes to do.

## PRESENT MOMENT

The first P of PRIDE is being in the present moment and the video gives you some activities you can use such as the concentration grid to help you and your athletes stay in the present.

> Living in the present moment or keeping your mind in the moment is one of the fundamental elements of success. In PRIDE there are videos and examples of people who have played in the present moment and what they look like when compared and contrasted with those who have not. If you can

learn to see when your players are in the moment and when they are not as a coach by establishing some "mental check points", you will be able to better help your players to unlock their potential and play at their best.

## PROCESS OVER OUTCOME
The second P discusses developing a process over an outcome- based approach. Cain gives examples of why it is important to focus on only the things you can control while letting go of and releasing the things you can't.

One of the major obstacles I see in athletics today is that people get too caught up in things that they can't control and when they do that, they beat themselves. The first law of sports psychology is don't beat yourself by focusing on things you can't control. Make the opponent beat you. The process section also discusses how you can structure practice so that you place a greater emphasis on the process and get your athletes to play with a process instead of outcome mentality.

## PERSPECTIVE/PHILOSOPHY
The third P discusses how we can develop a championship perspective and also the importance of knowing your WHY. Cain is a firm believer that all great performers have a very clear WHY.

When we have a big enough reason why, we can always find a way how. In this portion of the program you will learn how to get your athletes to refine and refocus their mission -- in other words, their "why?

## POSITIVE

The fourth P discusses how to maintain a positive mentality in a game where failure dominates.

> Being able to focus on what you want, rather than what you are trying to avoid is huge. This is a simple idea but it's not easy. Becoming more aware of the language you use when talking with yourself during practice or competition and using your self-talk to your advantage will allow you to unleash your potential and play to the best of your ability.

## PREPARATION

The fifth P is that of preparation. Cain agrees with coach John Wooden that failing to prepare is preparing to fail.

> Some of the best performers in the world including UFC champions, award-winning actors and top notch surgeons learn that having an hourglass system for preparation allows us be where we need to be when we need to be there, doing what we need to be doing in the moment, to allow us to get the most out of each moment. Preparation is an essential key to confidence, and learning how to properly prepare will keep you at your best when it is needed the most.

## ROUTINES

One of the best ways to play at your best on a consistent basis is to develop performance routines. Cain felt that it was important to dedicate a section of PRIDE to teaching you how to develop your own performance routine.

Habits and routines lead to familiarity. Familiarity leads to confidence. Any coach or player knows how critical confidence is to success. Routines are the life jacket of peak performance. In-game routines allow you to "have something to go to" when the pressure is on, your back is against the wall and you feel like your heart will pound out of your chest. Frequently, action is happening within the game so fast that there is no time for thinking, analysis or anything besides instant response using well practiced routines. Pre-game and pre-practice routines give you something to go to that will help you to get centered and in the moment and in-game routines help you to slow the game down. We are a product of our routines; unfortunately, many coaches and athletes don't know how to best structure productive routines.

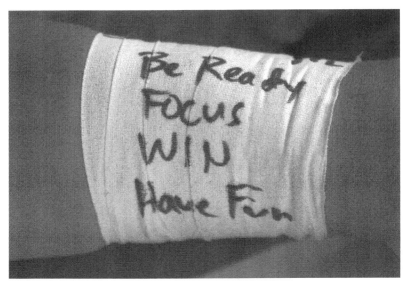

## RESPONSE-ABILITY

Choosing one's own way or making the choice to take response-ability is a common trait among peak performers.

Victor Frankel, in his great book *Man's Search For Meaning* tells the story of living through hell on earth, how he was able to be one of the few who survived the Nazi Concentration Camps during WWII. Frankel discusses how everything can be taken from a man except the last of his freedoms -- the ability to choose his own way or his ability to choose his attitude in every situation.

We use the three words, "Compared to what?" when talking about response-ability. Sometimes we get frustrated instead of fascinated with adversity and give away our response-ability too easily because we think we are up against insurmountable odds or too tough of a challenge. Compared to what Victor

Frankel went through, most of us reading this book have it pretty easy.

## RELAX & RECOVER

The ability to relax is a skill just like being able to execute the fundamentals of your sport. PRIDE takes you through the step-by-step process of learning how to train people in the relaxation response.

Similar to how you would start your concentration grid training in a quiet and controlled environment, building up to working on your "C-GRID" in a more chaotic and game-like environment, we have to be able to relax and recover in a quiet and controlled environment before we will be able to relax in the face of game like pressure. Unfortunately, a lot of coaches scream at players to "relax" in pressure situations. When this happens the players tense up more because now they know that you know they are out of control. Encouraging them to "breathe" as a way to relax and recover will be more productive than telling them to relax.

## RECOGNIZE–RELEASE–REFOCUS

Giving athletes the skills necessary to recognize where they are at mentally and the skills necessary to be able to release their mental bricks helping them to refocus on the moment is critical to consistent performance.

One of the things that Ken Ravizza, my mental game mentor, hammered home to his students was the importance of being able to "flush-it" and release when things don't go the athletes' way. Once athletes are able to recognize what's going on around them, and they realize that they are carrying mental bricks, they can release those bricks, check in on their body language and regroup while they shift their focus to WIN – What's Important Now.

## INTELLIGENCE

Cain believes that the statement "There is power in knowledge" is misleading. He feels that the real power lies not in knowledge, but that the ultimate power is in taking action.

Intelligence is overrated. There are a lot of people who know what to do but don't do what they know, so they never improve and are no better off than the person who does not know what to do. An example is when Rodger Banister broke the 4 minute mile and then this guy, call him Steve (who was a world class athlete, but LAZY) contacted Banister's coach and got the program that Banister followed for a year leading up to his record time.

On day one Steve ran the same pre-test as Banister and he smoked Banister's time by almost 4 seconds. Steve was so excited about having Banister's program and shattering his pre-test mile time that he showed everyone he could break the mile barrier as well. The only problem was that he did not USE Banister's program for the rest of the year. He just HAD the program. He had the knowledge, but did not apply the knowledge. Remember, K-A=0. Knowledge minus Action gets you Nothing. ACTION is what counts. Coaches and athletes need to stop using the answer "I know" and start showing what they know on a daily basis.

## IMAGERY

The use of mental imagery as a way to help improve performance is one of the most researched and demonstrated principles of peak performance. When you can vividly imagine something, you increase your chances of actually being able to execute that which you imagine.

The brain cannot tell the difference between what you mentally imagine and what you physically do. The two experiences are processed with very similar psychoneuromuscular pathways. So, from a mental perspective, what is imagined is true and real. Consequently by imagining, you are essentially creating the blueprint for your future real performances. Many athletes will imagine their performance the night before, seeing themselves performing exactly as they want to. The image they get is much like that you would see on TV or what they would see if they were actually performing. They build in all the senses and make the experience as real as possible.

While all of this is true, this is not Disneyland. Just because something is imagined, doesn't guarantee that it will come true. ACTION MUST BE TAKEN -- the physical work as well as mental imagery. The more imagery that the athlete performs the more confidence he builds, and the more confidence he builds, the better his performance will be. On the other hand, if the physical work is not done, the athlete will set-up for failure no matter how much mental game work she has done.

## INSPIRATION

Consider these questions: Do thoughts become things – TBT? Do we become what we surround ourselves with? That is what the research shows. The thoughts and images that run through our minds on a daily basis play a large role in determining what and who we become.

People always ask me if I think motivation is permanent. And to that I say, "no it isn't permanent." And because it isn't permanent, I recommended becoming surrounded with images, quotes, vision boards, posters and other things that symbolize what accomplishments are desired and what personal characteristics are to be acquired. I think it is essential that something is done to motivate and inspire action and accomplishment every day. Being surrounded with these images will inspire the achievement of greatness because thoughts become things and what is thought about is brought about.

Another key principal of motivation and inspiration is goal setting. Goals are roadmaps for accomplishment. Written goals are essential so that the mind has something real to focus upon because what the mind can imagine cannot be distinguished from reality. Writing goals on a bathroom mirror with a dry erase marker so they are seen multiple times a day will help to keep those goals in mind. Doing this simple exercise will help focus on what's important now to be accomplished.

## DEDICATION

Inspiration motivates. Setting goals fixates. Dedication perpetuates. Keeping a peak performance journal illuminates and cultivates the journey.

Keeping a peak performance journal in which goals are written down for the day before practice, what is learned that day is written down after practice and what needs to be worked on next is written down before the next practice is key for systematic athletic development. What gets measured, gets done. Quality progress will be routinely consistent.

Being dedicated to the team first and last as well as putting "we over me" is something that will help foster a great team environment.

Learning how to create an environment of dedication to team goals through establishing higher standards of excellence and core covenants is also a great way to increase dedication.

## DISCIPLINE

Discipline is a habit. Unfortunately so is a lack of discipline. Discipline is a skill that can be taught and practiced. Cain offered some tips on developing the skill of discipline.

One way in which discipline can be developed is to force action to occur that is different from feelings. This is important because so often things are not done because people don't feel like doing them. This is simply laziness getting the best of us. To combat this, select three things in your daily life that aren't being done that should be and challenge yourself to make them routine parts of your day. They can be things that a person may have to wake up five minutes earlier to be able to do. Something as simple as waking up five minutes earlier to accomplish those tasks is purely a matter of discipline, and in completing those daily tasks better all-around discipline can be developed.

Randy Mazey, a coach at Texas Christian University, has his players make their bed, shave and wear their seat belts -- three things that anyone can do on a daily basis to help develop the skill of discipline. Learning how to fake it until you make it, forcing yourself to act different than how you feel and having a system for developing disciplined eating and sleeping habits will pay dividends in helping you be at your best when it means the most.

## EXCELLENCE

Excellence is being at your best when it means the most, every single day. This has as much or more to do with mental strength than it does with physical skill.

Obviously, the greater the physical skills an athlete has, the greater her chance for success. However, there are plenty of athletes and teams that fall short of their potential because they learn too late in their career that practices are usually 90% physical and 10% mental, whereas games are 90% mental and 10% physical. Finding a way to build more of the mental game into practice is one of the fundamental steps in improving performance in the face of adversity and competition.

Having a system and structure in place to develop the mental part of the game in practice will help to achieve excellence. Helping coaches and athletes come closer to their potential with peak performance training through doing a-little-a-lot rather than a-lot-a-little and using the information contained in the PRIDE program on a routine and consistent basis will deliver the best chance for success.

## UFC CHAMPION SHARES SUCCESS STORY

The PRIDE DVD edition contains a special bonus interview that Brian Cain did with Ultimate Fighting Championship Welterweight Champion Georges St. Pierre. Cain and St. Pierre discuss various elements of peak performance and how they help St. Pierre perform at his best each and every time the cage door slams shut. *To obtain the PRIDE DVD program the please visit www.briancain.com.*

> Visit www.ToiletsBricksFishHooksAndPride.com
> For FREE Extras, Updates & Information

# CHAPTER 4 | THE SALESMAN WHO BEAT YOU EVERYTIME

Buying In To Peak Performance

One of the questions I often get from coaches is, "How do I get athletes to buy into peak performance training?" I have found that one of the best ways is to give them easy to use and remember tips and techniques that become a part of a program's overall vocabulary.

Some of the most effective peak performance tools I have used are simple acronyms and that people can remember that go on t-shirts, locker room walls and oddly enough on athletes bodies as tattoos. The following are examples of acronyms I suggest using:

## E+R=O

Many coaches and athletes fail to take responsibility for their careers and fall short of their goals and true potential. One way that I have had success in getting people to take responsibility is to get them to understand the formula E+R=O.

E+R=O stands for Events + Response = Outcome. Most people look to specific events that have caused them a lack of success. Examples of what I mean by this are a teammate that made an error, an umpire that missed a call, and a coach that did not give enough playing time. While those things may play a role, ultimately it's the athlete's RESPONSE to those events that determines what the final outcome will be.

## TODAY + TODAY + TODAY = YOUR CAREER

In their game changing book *Heads Up Baseball: Playing The Game One Pitch At A Time*, Ken Ravizza and Tom Hanson talk about how a career is really the sum of all todays. A lot of athletes I work with get caught up in counting the days to the "big game" or just going through the motions of practice thinking that they are a "gamer" and can turn it on when it counts and get the job done. Players and coaches need to understand that success in sport is not about counting the days, but making the days count. The goal is to work to get better every day and let the results take care of themselves. In most sports, you don't have control over the results. All you have control over is your performance. Generally speaking, if you play well and work the process, the end results will take care of themselves.

## RUN THE MARATHON

Rod Delmonico, former University of Tennessee head baseball coach, had a sign in his office that said "Run The Marathon." The sign served as a reminder to his players that the game of baseball is a marathon made up of a series of sprints combined with a continuous boxing match. Baseball is played over a long season compared with most other sports. Major League Baseball has 162 games in the season often played many weeks without a day off. Compare that with any other professional sport such a football that is played once a week and you will understand why I say that the goal is to be there in the moment today playing steadily on a day to day and pitch to pitch basis. Players that ride the roller coaster of emotions get caught up in the pace of the game and find themselves sprinting to stay ahead, which is not sustainable.

## GET BIG!

I often talk to athletes about the importance of body language and what kind of message their body language communicates to others about their confidence and self-belief. We spend a lot of time talking about walking with a swagger and being big. Your psychology will affect your physiology and your physiology will affect your psychology. By watching the way a person walks and listening to a way a person talks tells you a lot about that person's belief in getting the job done. Having big body language helps with self-confidence, even if you are faking it until you make it.

## CHECK- IN

Athletes that perform at their best when their best is needed have learned to live in the present moment and to continually feed themselves with positive self-talk and positive imagery. The term "check-in" is used daily in my communications with athletes as a reminder for them to check-in on their self-talk, body language and thoughts. All athletes will have negative self-talk (self-criticism) and negative images running through their minds when they are faced with the failure that is inevitable in sport. The best players are the ones that check-in pitch-by-pitch and can get back on track after they get derailed.

## FLUSH-IT

Athletes that can let go of mistakes and get back to the next play or pitch are going to have a better chance of winning than those athletes that beat themselves up over previous mistakes. Skip Bertman, the former head baseball coach at Louisiana State University, was one of the first coaches in college baseball to encourage his players to "flush it" after a bad at-bat. Because of Skip, you will now find symbolic flushing toilet banks in many dugouts around the country. Players need to be able to focus on playing the game one pitch at a time and if they are continually thinking about previous pitches, at-bats, or even worse, previous games, they are not in the present moment and are not playing one pitch at a time.

You can invest in your own "flush-it" toilet bank or "flush-it" foam toilet at *www.briancain.com* to help your athletes flush the past and get onto the next play or pitch.

## RELEASE YOUR MENTAL BRICKS

How much does a 3-3/4" x 2-1/2" x 8" standard brick weigh? If you answered about 5 pounds, you would be correct. Now, if I asked you to carry a standard brick for five seconds, you probably could do it. Am I right? So, do you think you could carry the same brick for five minutes? Maybe? What about five hours? I guess, probably not?

As coaches and athletes, if we have a bad play, a bad day of practice or a bad game, we carry a lot of mental bricks. Those mental bricks build up, weigh on us and zap our energy similar to what it may be like to physically carrying a brick for five minutes or five hours. Releasing our mental bricks is another part of the peak performance language to help players to be able to get themselves back into the present moment and to be able to let go of the failure and negativity that is built into competition.

## MOOMBA DISEASE

MOOMBA disease is one of the most deadly diseases a coach or athlete can catch. Discovered by my friend and mentor Ed Agresta, MOOMBA disease is highly contagious and can ruin a team. The only good thing about MOOMBA disease is that it is 100% self-inflicted and curable. MOOMBA is an acronym for My Only Obstacle May Be ATTITUDE. I truly believe that it is attitude that will ultimately determine the altitude of success reached in sport and that attitude is a decision. Attitudes are contagious. Is yours worth catching?

The attitude you choose is a matter of responsibility. If I am working with a team and sense that a player has caught this deadly MOOMBA disease, I will take a photo of a small little creature and write the word MOOMBA on it and place it in the player's helmet or locker. When they get that photo, they know that they must check in and make an attitude adjustment before they will find the success they are looking for.

## ACE

At the elite high school and college level, most coaches and athletes have dedicated their entire lives to their sport. When people are that dedicated to something, they have a tendency to personalize performance and see their self-worth as linked to their performance results. But what if their performance wasn't connected to their status as an athlete, coach or even human being? What if their performance was an act?

What most people may not realize is that it's healthy to see yourself as more than just a coach or an athlete and to not personalize performance. Your self-worth should not come from how you play.

It's okay to be an actor. What is an actor? A great actor forces herself to act differently from how she feels. When she steps into the arena that is her role, she must ACT the role that she is supposed to play and not necessarily the role that she may feel like playing.

When you commit to ACTING you will realize that Acting Changes Everything -- ACE. If you are ten for ten or zero for ten at the plate as a softball player, you should act the same way when you walk to the plate. If you are the number one pitcher on the team or the number twelve pitcher, you should approach your bullpen with the same type of mental focus. That is acting. Great players act as if it is impossible to fail. Michael Jordan, the basketball superstar of the Chicago Bulls, said it best when he talked about learning to carry himself like an All-American before he was an All-American at the University of North Carolina because that was going to help his performance and increase his chances of becoming an All-American. Don't wait until you get the accolades or the recognition to start acting confident. Act confident before you get the accolades and recognition and you'll increase your chances of performing well enough to deserve those honors. As Dr. Rob Gilbert taught me, remember your ABC's. And here's another ABC to remember: Always Behave Confidently -- ABC.

## GOYA

Another phrase taught to me by my friend and mentor Ed Agresta was Get Off Your Anatomy -- GOYA. All players can go through the motions of just getting through a day. It happens to the best of us. When you catch yourself or a teammate falling into that trap, you must remember to GOYA. Early morning weight training sessions, evening runs, and academic study time all can require a little motivational speech from yourself and a reminder that if you want to reach your full potential, you must GOYA.

## WIN

Everyone knows the importance of playing the game one-play-at-a-time and living in the present moment. If you truly want to win, you must focus on What's Important Now! What's important now is THIS PLAY. And what's important now is THIS PAGE in the book. Have you been reading this book with the intensity and purpose of finding something that you could take and use immediately? Were you totally engrossed in the moment with the words on this page? If you were, please accept my congratulations on being able to get "LOCKED-IN". If you were not, remember that WINNING is a byproduct of being where you need to be when you need to be there. Being in the present moment play-by-play for the marathon or for the entire game is what will give you the best chance for success.

Visit www.ToiletsBricksFishHooksAndPride.com
For FREE Extras, Updates & Information

# CHAPTER 5 | BREATHING AN OSCAR

Fake it Until You Make it

Having emerged as one of the best peak performance coaches for college athletic programs as well as mixed martial arts fighters, Brian Cain shared his insight about working with these two very different groups of athletes.

I've been comparing mixed martial arts (MMA) ultimate fighters with collegiate level athletic teams that I have worked with for many years. Many aspects of both groups are very similar. The major difference is that in most collegiate sports if you lose a competition, you are required to mentally rebound quickly for the next game, which in most cases may be held within a few days or a week while in MMA, if you lose, you have the mental challenge of stewing over what went wrong for months before you have the opportunity to fight again.

Both MMA and collegiate athletics have advantages and disadvantages with their various time constraints. College athletes have the advantage of getting immediate feedback from real opponents to the many different athletic approaches they may take to gain a victory. On the other hand, they have the disadvantage of having relatively little time to assess what went wrong and to master new approaches. MMA fighters have the opposite challenge. They have a lot of time to assess what went wrong and to practice potential solutions, but very little time to gain

authentic feedback from real opponents to perfect their athletic approaches. Of the two groups of athletes, college teams probably have more to gain by studying and practicing the strategies and tactics of the MMA fighters. For one, they have more time constraints facing them and two, there are many more of them than MMA fighters.

Having worked with the top teams in college baseball, softball, ice hockey, lacrosse, basketball, football, swimming and diving, golf, tennis, soccer, and the best fighters in the world, Cain feels that many coaches and athletes could benefit from a better understanding of what goes into the mental training that the most fierce competitors on the planet use almost every day.

> When the MMA fighter steps into the octagon, it is much more than a simple competition. It's war. Both fighters are trying to take possession of the cage and part of how they do that is through

presenting a supremely confident demeanor – what I call 'Get Big or Championship Body Language.' Translated, that means they present themselves in a manner calculated to intimidate their opponent, acting in a manner usually much more confident than they actually feel.

All the fighters that I work with get nervous before a fight – mentally going through some second-guessing, fear, and regret about having to go into the cage. The fighters who win know how to 'get their butterflies to fly in formation', so to speak.

In many sports at the college level, you can tell who is winning by the way the winning athletes walk around on the sidelines with a certain swagger, shall we say? Anyone can. It's all in the body language. When coaching the athletes I work with, I always ask, 'whose field is this?'; or 'who owns this court?'; or 'whose home plate is it?' Believing that you own the field or are going to take possession of it is one of the first steps in developing an aggressive and competitive mindset.

## FAKE IT UNTIL YOU MAKE IT

Both the MMA fighters and college athletes get nervous and anxious before a big competition. The key is for them to let their actions dictate their feelings and not the other way around.

Athletes who can 'act' as if they are what they hope they will be have a much better chance of performing at or near their best than those who allow themselves to fall into the trap of acting how they feel. When they act as if it's impossible to fail, or act as if they are the best fighter or player in the world for that moment and carry themselves with that absolute certainty of confidence, sooner or later they will start to feel like that self-assured warrior going out to do battle. Faking it will help them to find the energy or emotion needed, and faking it will also help them to get the results they are looking for.

Another way of looking at 'faking it' is it's much easier for athletes to talk themselves into feeling than it is for them to feel themselves into action. Specifically, if they wait around until the impulse arises within them to go to the cage, take extra shots, rise up and swing again beyond their limits, or push themselves further in the weight room, that urge may never come. They have to ACT like they want to get their body charging so that their brains will follow. **It's the start that stops most people** because the stimulus they are waiting for never comes when they want it to or never comes at all.

## MAJOR LEAGUE PITCHER AND MOVIE STAR SHARE SIMILAR EXPERIENCES

Cal State Fullerton alum and actor Kevin Costner said it best in a conversation with ESPN's Kyle Peterson during a pitching change in an NCAA Super Regional Game between Cal State Fullerton and the University of Arizona.

There are days when you show up and you don't feel

like acting, but you have to fake-it so that sooner or later you find it and the universe opens up for you. On such days you realize that 'faking it' really is enabling you to relax because when you're relaxed, you can fully focus on the job at hand.

Peterson compared that analogy to going out to the mound, not feeling his best, but acting as if he had his best stuff, so as not to tip off his opponents. He might feel at his best 10% of the time and feel terrible 10% of the time, but it's the 80% where he goes to battle with his mental skills to help him fake it until he finds it, that made him a winner. Most of the time when he would fake it, sooner or later his good stuff would show up. The point is, however, that if he didn't fake it, it would probably never show up.

It's amazing how well this mental strategy works for so many athletes in so many sports. Faking it until you make it is one of the most effective skills employed by mentally tough athletes.

## PERFORMANCE AWARENESS ALARM CRITICAL FOR SUCCESS

One way in which Brian Cain gets athletes to increase their awareness about when they are inadvertently sabotaging themselves with destructive thoughts or mentally wandering off the reservation is to use what he calls the Awareness Alarm.

I have athletes use a wristwatch or a cell phone and

set an alarm to go off every 20 minutes of their waking hours. What they're supposed to do when the alarm goes off is to check in on one of their mental toughness goals that we've setup together.

For example, if I'm working with an athlete that doesn't carry herself with confidence, I will have her say out loud, 'Confidence is a choice, and my choice is that I will carry myself like a champion and become a champion.' I will have her repeat this every 20 minutes when her alarm goes off. After a few days, the athlete should be walking around with a much more confident body language. At first when she starts doing this, what you will see is that the alarm will go off and the athlete will check in, become aware that her body language is less than ideal (what I call the loser's limp) and will respond by straightening up, throwing her shoulders back and "Getting Big" as she walks around.

Now we all know that body language alone will not make a champion, but we also know that if an athlete doesn't have confident body language, she is defeating herself and will fall short of her potential."

## BREATHING IS CRITICAL TO PERFORMING WELL

If you have ever watched The Ultimate Fighter Reality Show on Spike TV, you may have seen an episode in which UFC Welterweights Matt Serra and Matt Hughes were the coaches. Some of the most prominent coaching words used by the Team Serra corner during any of their fights were "breathe, relax and breathe". Brian Cain contends that the interesting insight here is that fighters and athletes in all sports beat themselves by not being able to breathe in the heat of competition. Cain says he has personally witnessed this, "time and time again."

I had the chance to be cage side when Georges St. Pierre fought Josh Koscheck at UFC 74. I was impressed with how often St. Pierre's coaches including Greg Jackson, Phil Nurse and Firas Zahabi were saying, 'Breathe Georges. Relax and take good deep breaths.' It goes to show that even in the most fierce and competitive sport on the planet, the best of the best are still working on breathing and self-regulation, even during a fight. Now breathing may not sound like a very challenging action for what we humans need to do. After all, we are very good at breathing since we do it all the time and we even do it without being aware of it much of the time. In the heat of competitive battle, however, healthy breathing is not normal. In fact, for the most part it is catch-as-catch-can – short, erratic, frequently interrupted and often done too often or not often enough. It is common for athletes to hold their breath in competition which will sabotage all the benefits of their conditioning. Healthy breathing is very difficult to do in the heat of battle, so it must be learned and deliberately practiced.

Matt Serra said the same thing on The Ultimate Fighter reality show. In Ultimate Fighting as in other sports, there are no little things. It can be one shot, one play, one pitch or one punch that can make the difference in the outcome. You have to stay in the present moment, one punch, one play or one pitch at a time and you do that by consciously and conscientiously breathing.

It is no surprise that the greatest coaches in the world are talking as much if not more about breathing than they are about fundamentals and strategies in competition. George Horton at The University of Oregon, Dave Serrano at Cal State Fullerton, Patrick Murphy at The University of Alabama, Jim Schlossnagle at Texas Christian University, Gary Gilmore at Coastal Carolina, Tim Corbin at Vanderbilt are always talking about breathing and staying in the moment. What I am learning as I gain more experience working with Olympic athletes, top college coaches and athletes, professional baseball players and ultimate fighters is that the best of the best in any sport are always talking about breathing and staying in the moment. I think that it's no secret why they also W.I.N., focus on **W**hat's **I**mportant **N**ow.

Visit www.ToiletsBricksFishHooksAndPride.com
For FREE Extras, Updates & Information

# CHAPTER 6 | TAKE A LOOK INSIDE. SEE WHAT YOU FIND.

There Is Only There If You Can See It

When athletes have performance awareness, it allows them to recognize when they get out-of-sync mentally or mechanically and allows them to make in-game adjustments. The best players at all levels are able to do this pitch-to-pitch and are thus able to play more consistently and have more success.

I vividly remember being at Cal State Fullerton sitting in a graduate school course in The Philosophy of Sport taught by my mentor and author of *Heads Up Baseball: Playing The Game One Pitch At A Time*, Dr. Ken Ravizza. He put this photo on the board and started talking about getting athletes to look inside of themselves for the answers and for what they want– self-coaching and developing performance awareness. That one class changed my approach to coaching and changed my life.

## TAKE A LOOK INSIDE

When you take a look inside and ask yourself why you do what you do and what your mission or purpose is, you can often find a motivation that can't be created by an outside source. I truly believe that coaches can motivate players and vice-versa, and that the strongest form of motivation comes from looking inside oneself and asking WHY?

Harvey Dorfman, author of *The Mental Game of Baseball*, shared with me that to get athletes to change, there is a three step process that they should follow:

1. Development of awareness
2. Having a strategy to improve performance
3. Implementation of the strategy

The player who has poor body language when faced with adversity most likely doesn't have the awareness that he is carrying himself with the loser's limp when things don't go his way, and most likely would change this if he had awareness. Using videos to show the player his body language when faced with adversity can be a great asset.

## WATCHING VIDEOS CAN SPEED UP AWARENESS

I remember the last pitch I threw in the summer of 1997 before I arrived on campus at the University of Vermont (UVM). I was pitching at a field in Keene, New Hampshire and the lighting was not great. The last pitch I threw was hit for a line drive right back at me like a bullet. Lucky for me I got my glove arm up in front of my face at the last second and blocked the ball with my forearm before my face was seriously injured. I got a lucky bounce close to me, so I picked up the ball and threw the batter out at first, one of the best plays I made that day or maybe ever.

Two weeks later when we had an intra-squad scrimmage at UVM, our pitching coach at the time kept telling me, "You aren't finishing. You aren't following through. Do you feel that?" Truthfully, I couldn't really feel anything because the movements in athletics are instinctive and often so fast that often you can't feel anything or notice what your body is doing. You don't really have time to think about what's happening, much of the time. You just react when plays get under way. In response to my coaches question, I also never worked on developing a feel or awareness so whenever I was asked if I could feel something, I responded with a "yes" because I didn't want to disappoint the coach or feel like an idiot.

About midway through the fall season I watched a video of myself throwing in an intra-squad scrimmage. I noticed that I was not finishing the pitch, but rather getting my hands up in front of my face much like a boxer would to cover up during a barrage of punches from an opponent. I was stunned at how I had not noticed doing this at all from the inside looking out. It appeared as if I was trying to protect myself from getting hit again with a line drive. Seeing this on video, a light bulb went off for me, and I was instantly able to make the change in my delivery and not so coincidently started to have more success.

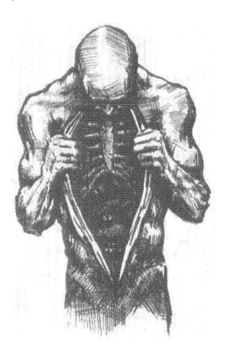

I was recently working with a top college program and was observing a coach working with a few of his hitters. What I heard was very familiar. I heard the coach telling the hitter that his lower half was going first, but his upper body and hands were going too soon and the spring like action we try to create as hitters by exploding open with the lower half and letting the core upper body and hands follow, was not where it needed to be. The hitter then proceeded to do it correctly and the coach said, "Did you feel that?" The player said "yes."

I have never heard a player say to a coach, "no, I can't feel that" when asked. I've since learned that the better question to ask is, "Tell me what you feel." I've also learned that by asking the player to tell you what he feels, you then can get inside of the athlete's mind and let him start to develop awareness as to what's going on.

Think about asking more and saying less. When you ask open-ended questions such as "tell me what you felt" or "what was your thought process for that hitter," you put the responsibility on the athlete and start to develop them as players who can coach themselves and make in-game adjustments.

## THE FEDEX PHENOMENA

Getting a player to look inside is essential to their development as an athlete and as a person. I assume that you have seen a Federal Express logo before. My question is have you seen the arrow inside of the FedEx logo?

If not, take a close look between the E and the X. I am sure you will see it. Once you see it, from that moment until the day you die, you will always see the arrow in the Fed Ex logo. What I challenge you to do is have a paradigm shift, much like you did when you first saw the arrow. I want that paradigm shift for you to be getting athletes to look inside by asking more questions and giving fewer answers. Start to develop awareness so they can coach themselves and make more in-game adjustments.

Get your players to take a look inside and see the arrow that is inside of them and inside of the game. For you as a coach, take a look inside of yourself and inside of how you do things. Remember that the majority of the players you coach will not make a living playing sports, but instead will make a life using the mental skills you teach them on a daily basis.

Few players will come back 10 years after graduation and say. "Thanks for teaching me to hit the outside pitch, or "for how to defend the up and out route," but they will come back and say, "Thanks for teaching me to look inside at what's important to me and in my life and thanks for teaching me to find the "arrow" in those difficult situations where I would normally get frustrated." When you can shift from getting frustrated to getting fascinated and can do that by taking a look at what you can learn from each and every opportunity, you will truly be successful.

# CHAPTER 7 | HITTING THE TARGET MOST PEOPLE NEVER SEE

### Because It's All In The Process

Pretend that you are visiting a friend in Boston and it's your first time in the city. You arrive in Bean Town overwhelmed by the "Big Dig" detours, the one-way streets, and the traffic, on top of not having a clue where you're going. You remember that you have a map, but after an hour of going in circles, you decide the map is no help.

Instead, you call your friend for help and he tells you to, "Stay positive. You'll find it." Another hour passes and you're still lost. You call your friend again and he tells you to, "Keep working hard. You'll find it." Mumbling under your breath now about how much of a friend you really have, you punch the gas but soon realize you're getting lost twice as fast. The problem isn't in your ability to stay positive in the face of adversity or to work hard, the problem is that you're in Boston and you have a map of Chicago. You have the wrong map.

Often in sports we're told to work hard and be positive, but we leave our preparation, training, and performance to chance because we don't have a specific plan for improvement. In other words, we don't have the right map. The individuals and teams that win most often and have the most fun, play and practice like they're on a mission. There's a purpose and a strategy behind everything they do.

## PURPOSE OF GOAL SETTING – GOING ON A MISSION

As you think about your personal mission in sports, you should answer three critical questions:

1. Why do you play?
2. What would you like people to say about you and the way you played the game?
3. What do you want to accomplish in your sport?

## WHY ASK WHY?

Knowing why you play is critical because when you know why you play sports, it will help you battle through the inevitable hardships. When answering why you play, try to get as specific as possible. Answering that it's fun is important but too vague. Answering, "I love the head-to-head competition going against another competitor, the camaraderie of the team, and the challenge to be at my best every day," is much more specific and will provide you with more motivation and more of an operational set of targets.

## WHAT DO YOU WANT PEOPLE TO SAY ABOUT YOUR CAREER?

When you answer what you would like people to say about you, you may answer, "I'm a hard worker, I'm a great team player and I'm the kind of player that never quits." Once you decide what you would want people to say about you, you must do those things every day. If you want to be remembered as a person that worked extremely hard, you must work extremely hard today. Do you want to be remembered as a great teammate? What can you do to today to demonstrate that you are a great teammate? Does this mean communicating well, sharing ideas, and following team traditions?

## KEY QUESTIONS FOR GOAL SELECTION

Answering a few key questions will help you plan your mission and will serve as your road map to help accomplish your goals. Try writing down the answers to these key questions and sharing them with your teammates, coaches, parents, and others in your inner circle of support. Writing these down will also help cement your commitment to the goal.

1. What would you like to be able to do in your sport that you can't do now?

   Example: Consistently throw my fastball for strikes.

2.  How would your athletic performance improve
    when you achieve your goal?

    Example: I would get ahead in the count more
    often, I would walk fewer batters and as a result
    I would give my team a better chance to win.

3.  How long have you wanted the goal?

    Example: Ever since I saw the statistic that a
    surprisingly large amount of walks wind up as
    runs scored.

4.  What have you done to achieve what you want?

    Example: I've been charting my bullpen and
    practice sessions to see if I'm improving the
    accuracy of my pitching.

5.  What resources can you rely on — people who
    support you and places to go to get information?

    Example: I can rely on my coaches, teammates,
    videotapes and charts.

6.  What things may be holding you back that you're
    willing to sacrifice in order to help you achieve
    your goal?

    Example: I don't get enough practice throwing
    between games. I would be willing to sacrifice
    my personal time after practice to throw more
    quality pitches and to do more throwing
    visualization at night.

7. What will you accept as proof that you're achieving your goal?

   Example: I would accept walking fewer than two batters per nine innings pitched as proof that I was achieving my goal.

8. How would you describe your action plan for accomplishing your goal?

   Example: I would chart my practice and games and I would focus on throwing first pitch strikes. I would take a game like approach to practice by giving myself more game specific situations such as starting a batter with two balls and no strikes, so I'll have to deal with more realistic pressure to throw strikes.

Once you set a goal, remember that there are the three key steps to making that goal come to fruition.

1. Make a commitment.
2. Make it public.
3. Make it happen.

## GUIDELINES FOR GOING ON A MISSION:

1. *SET SPECIFIC AND MEASURABLE GOALS*
The first step to having a successful mission is targeting where you want to go and having a clear plan/map on how to get there (remember having a map of Chicago when you were in Boston didn't work). Give yourself specific performance goals such as: I want to get my first pitch in for a strike 80% of the time and I want to stay in control of myself on the mound, by following my pre-pitch routine and by breathing properly.

2. *SET PROCESS PROCEDURES, NOT OUTCOME GOALS*
Goals often center on outcomes such as becoming state champions or making the all-state team, which is important, but outcome goals should not be set ahead of process goals because we don't usually have control over outcome goals, whereas we do usually have control over process goals. Control is the key concept here. We need to focus on what we can control.

Let's say you want to hit .300 this season -- a specific and measurable outcome goal. Now ask yourself, "What do I need to do to hit .300?" Your answer is the process goal, the map directions to get you there. Your answer may come out something like, "I need to hit the ball consistently hard and I do that by having a pre-pitch routine that helps me stay in control and helps me to play one pitch at a time. If I do that, all the details of hitting .300 will take care of itself."

Or let's take the goal setting a step further: To hit the ball consistently hard, what do you need to do? Your answer might then be, "I need to swing at pitches that I can hit well." Then taking things to a greater level of detail: To swing at pitches that you can hit well, what do you need to do? "I need to be in control of myself at the plate. I need to recognize the pitch once it leaves the pitcher's hand, and focus on driving the ball where it is pitched."

Now if you make your goal driving the ball consistently hard, and swinging at pitches you can hit, don't you think that you'll have a better chance of hitting .300 than if you simply set the goal at hitting .300?

3. **SET POSITIVE GOALS**

At an early age, we are conditioned to think negatively at home by our parents and relatives. For example, do these commands sound familiar: "Don't touch the stove because you may get burned" or "Don't cross the street without looking both ways?" Have you ever heard these phrasings before? Of course you have. And with such commands so commonly repeated so many times, is it any wonder that we give ourselves commands such as: "Don't strikeout" or "Don't walk this batter"?

In contrast, what if we gave ourselves suggestions specifically about what we wanted to accomplish instead of what we wanted to avoid? For example, what if I gave myself suggestions such as, "I want to be aggressive in the strike zone," or "I want to throw a quality pitch to this hitter and get ahead?" Wouldn't these be much more productive than telling myself, "Don't walk this batter, or don't fall behind?"

Focus on what you want to have happen, not what you want to avoid. This is the foundation for positive thinking and a positive mental attitude.

#### 4. *SET SHORT, MEDIUM AND LONG RANGE GOALS*
Setting specific daily, weekly, and seasonal goals will also increase motivation and help the mind to focus on the short term actions that are more easily within reach of accomplishment. For example, "Today I am going to work on driving the ball the other way with power by letting the ball get deeper in the zone," or "This week I want to hit the ball the other way with more power in games by looking for a good pitch to go the other way with," or "This season I want to raise my batting average 50 points by staying in control of myself with my routine and by swinging at pitches that are within my plan."

#### 5. *READJUST YOUR GOALS*
Readjusting goals when necessary can be valuable; it keeps motivation high and focused on improvement. For example, a pitcher who wants to get ahead and stay ahead of the count beginning with the first strike for 70% of the hitters she faces but is already getting ahead of 68% of hitters will

lose focus because the goal is too easy to reach. This pitcher may want to readjust her goal to get ahead of the hitters 80% of the time or greater by the end of the season to keep herself motivated on a daily basis.

6. *FOSTER A COMMITMENT TO YOUR GOALS AND SET UP A SUPPORT SYSTEM*

Lou Holtz, the iconic NCAA football coach, said that there are two reasons why he became successful, "I have a great spouse and I am very goal oriented." Holtz was known for setting daily goals and for surrounding himself with people who believed in him making up his strong support system.

Great coaches and athletes communicate with each other, their teammates, family, and friends about their goals. By surrounding yourself with people who believe in what you're trying to accomplish, you will be able to count on their support if and when you find yourself struggling, and athletics can usually be counted on to deliver a struggle at some point. It will never be perfect and it will never be easy.

To achieve success, coaches and athletes should develop a specific, measurable, positively phrased, challenging plan of action to improve their performance, and most importantly, they should work at it TODAY!

Visit www.ToiletsBricksFishHooksAndPride.com
For FREE Extras, Updates & Information

# CHAPTER 8 | PRACTICING THE TERRIBLE

S peak with ten baseball coaches on the topics of batting stance, pitching mechanics or strength training, and you are likely to hear ten different responses. Should the hitter start with an open stance and stride towards the pitcher, or should the hitter start and finish with a closed stance? Let's consider two situations when the count is three and one with a runner on first base. First, automatically send the runner, thus turning it into a hit and run situation because you are confident that your hitter, if the pitch is a strike, will get a good piece of the ball; or second, instruct the runner to play the three and one pitch just like any other, with a three-step lead off the base and good secondary extension.

There are many different philosophies on the strategic and mechanical aspects of the game. There is no right or wrong way, just different ways depending on what part of the game you're in, how much pressure there is to score and whom you ask. There is one necessary aspect or strategy that any little league or professional baseball coach will agree upon. It is that quality practice is essential for any team to have the best chance for competitive success.

## PRACTICE MAKES PERMANENT
Ken Ravizza and Tom Hanson write in *Heads-Up Baseball* that a player's career is the sum of all todays. Assuming this is true, there is quite possibly no other factor as important in the pursuit of excellence as quality practice.

Ballplayers spend many more hours on the practice field than in competition. Practice does not make perfect, practice makes permanent, and quality practice gives you the best chance for quality performance.

If you have talent, you have an advantage, but you are not guaranteed success. How many times does the athlete with the most "natural talent" end up losing or not performing well? Whether the "natural talent" does or does not exist, there is not much a coach can do to change it. That's why it becomes essential that coaches focus their time and energy in an area that they have control over -- quality practice.

## FAILING TO PREPARE IS PREPARING TO FAIL

Legendary UCLA Basketball coach John Wooden said that it often took him twice as long to prepare for a practice as it actually did to run it. This being said, one of the most important aspects of quality practice is the time and energy spent by the coach in preparing for the day's practice. If Wooden is to be believed, failing to prepare for a quality practice may be preparing to fail.

The first step in preparing for a quality practice is assessing the needs of the team by evaluating previous practice and performance. What are the players' strengths and weaknesses, and what can be done to improve them? After an assessment is made, it becomes critical to establish goals for each individual practice. Knowing what is to be accomplished will increase motivation, minimize stress, provide direction, increase intensity, add meaning to workouts, lay down a basis for post-practice evaluation, and provide a strong foundation to build upon.

## DETAILED PRACTICE PLAN

A critical component of quality practice is having a detailed practice plan. Spending the time before practice to prepare will minimize stress levels because it is clear what needs to be accomplished and when. Preparing for practice ahead of time also increases motivation, intensity, direction, and time management. Incorporating activities in practice that are in line with pre-practice goals and objectives will help set the stage for quality practice.

A detailed practice plan should consist of clock time, for example 5:00 pm to 5:15 pm, as well as the time it will take to complete the activity, for example 15 minutes. Creating clear activity boundaries will allow players and coaches to know how much time they will have to practice, so they can make the most efficient use of their time. The activity should also have a specific name, such as front toss or quick hands, so that players and coaches will recognize it, remember it, and communicate about it more easily. Having a diagram of the facility with an outline of where the different drills or stations will happen, a chart with the players' names and specific rotations of where they should be at a given time will help in time management as well. Each player will be accounted for and will be held responsible for knowing where they should be at all times.

Writing down the specific equipment – the number of balls and bats, what speed the pitching machine should be set at and the type of pitch will also help to eliminate confusion or last minute scrambling. Equally important is incorporating time for equipment set up and take down, transition between activities, and water breaks. Posting the practice plan as soon as possible, so that the players can see what is expected of them, will allow them to prepare mentally. Players can start to use their imagery and visualization skills to see themselves performing the way they want to that day in practice. Sticking to the practice plan and keeping practice to the specified time will help to minimize stress for players who may have academic or social commitments after practice.

## GOAL SETTING CARDS

Players often spend time warming up their muscles and bodies for practice, but rarely spend time getting their minds warmed up and where they need to be for a quality practice. A technique that I have found effective is incorporating pre-practice goal setting into a warm-up routine.

Pre-practice goal setting begins by handing all players an index card and having everyone write their goal for the practice that day on the card. Each player must then turn in their card to their positional coach before they start practice so that the coach can see what they are working on. Some sample goals are: to be more confident, to work on refocusing during practice when they catch themselves drifting away, to throw good low strikes in the pen, or to aggressively hit to the opposite field in batting practice. Doing all of this allows coaches to have a baseline for what each player thinks they need to work on to improve. It also lets the coach see who is mentally prepared for practice, and who has not taken responsibility for their preparation.

## DRILL PURPOSE TEST

Sometimes coaches wrongly assume that their players understand why they've been asked to do a specific drill or what the objectives of that drill really are. A way to check and see if players know the purpose of a specific drill is simply by handing them a drill purpose test and having them individually write what they feel the purpose of the drill is. Coaches are often surprised when they read what players think the purpose of a drill is. When the players know what it is they are working on with each specific drill, the opportunity for quality practice is greatly enhanced.

## PRE-PRACTICE TIME

A technique that is often used to help players focus on practice is to give them five to ten minutes before practice to joke around, play games with teammates such as flip, two ball, and pepper, or to let them do whatever they need to do to get mentally ready. Building this time into practice serves the function of transitioning smoothly from class or work to practice by getting the social aspect out of the way so that they can focus on a quality practice. Team socializing is a critical part of the teambuilding process as it allows time for players who may not often see each other off the diamond to interact and communicate about things outside of baseball.

## GLASS OF WATER DEMONSTRATION

A technique used to help get players centered and focused for practice is to help them quiet the mind of all thoughts not relevant to the present moment, the present practice. Athletes are asked to shut their eyes and imagine their minds are like a glass of water fresh from the tap and loaded with cloudy air bubbles. When everyone has begun imagining, players are then asked to inhale deeply through their nose and from the belly, exhaling slowly through the mouth, trying to imagine that with each breath their minds are becoming clearer and clearer just like the water in the glass.

This process may only take a minute or two but will pay large dividends. It allows players and coaches to get reacquainted with the idea that there is nothing they can do about the past, it is already over, and there is nothing they can do about the future until practice is over. It also reconnects them with the importance of the moment and that the time is now and the place is here.

## SILENT PRACTICE
A technique to help players get focused during practice is to use silent practice. Silent practice is just that – silent. There is no talking by the players. This exercise takes anywhere from five to eight minutes. The players are asked to be as quiet as possible, enhancing the environment for them to focus on the task at hand and get mentally prepared for practice. Coaches should make it a point to inform the players that silent practice is not punishment. Rather it's a technique to help them learn to focus. This technique is also beneficial for coaches during a season because instead of wasting valuable practice time confronting the team about their inability to focus, the coach simply informs the team that they are not as present and focused as they need to be and thus will be conducting silent practice for the next five minutes. This can be done in any practice situation where verbal communication is not a priority.

## 30-SECOND-DRILL

The 30-second-drill is used to demonstrate to players that if they are willing to take responsibility, they have the ability to control their levels of attention and focus at any given moment. Players are first asked to commit to giving 30 seconds of totally undivided attention. Most will be able to do so. When a coach says go, the players will all do something different from what they were doing just five seconds before and "lock-in" on what is being directed.

Players are then asked to notice how the energy level in the group is different from what it was ten seconds ago. This is what quality practice is all about. It's about catching attention when it drifts, and bringing it back to the present moment by using the 30-second-drill. When 30 seconds is up, players are allowed to relax. When they have relaxed, the coach asks them what they each did to turn themselves around and to "lock-in"?

The 30-second-drill also helps coaches when they notice that players are not focusing as much as they need to. By informing players that they need to give 30 seconds, it will let them know that their coach recognizes that they are not as focused as they need to be. This also helps, in a time-out, pre or post-game talk, when coaches are going to make a critical point and want everyone's attention. 30-second-drills are typically used five to ten times a day, and work well to keep all planned activities within the planned time frame. If the 30 second talk goes on too long, messages lose their effectiveness.


## VIDEO TAPE PRACTICE

Visual images are very powerful and efficient in communicating ideas. Most of us believe that a picture is figuratively, if not literally, worth a thousand words. Many of us are visual learners, especially in this day and age when video technology, television and computers are so prevalent. Using videotape to analyze and model behavior not only works as an effective teaching tool of athletic skills and mechanics, it also serves as a motivator and a good teacher of the mental game.

Most athletes enjoy watching themselves on video, especially when they are performing well. Developing a personal highlight DVD from practice or games in which the player performed well can give the player a constant positive image that they can use to help with their imagery. Many times when a player is in a slump and they are asked to form a mental image of themselves the last time they were performing well, it is difficult, if not impossible to do well. Viewing videos of the player performing well can help a player in a slump to regain her confidence. Unfortunately, many players pick out only the negative things when they watch. It's up to the coach to emphasize what they are doing well more than what the player is doing poorly.

## GAME LIKE SIMULATION
Although it is difficult to mirror the intensity, adversity and pressure of an actual competition in practice, there are exercises that coaches can run to make the practice environment more game-like. Some of these techniques to enhance practice include keeping score, using situational simulation, having and using practice uniforms, and creating consequences for the losing team.

Another way to simulate game like situations is to practice overcoming adversity by doing what is sometimes called "throwing in the monkeys." This is an expression describing unexpected actions that influence game conditions such as manipulating the scoring, making unfavorable calls, and changing game conditions. These are situations that are calculated to test the psychological readiness of the team to handle adversity. Adverse situations can often hit during a game raising frustration levels and tempers, causing a team to fold or start pointing fingers at umpires, fans, or teammates.

Coaches should advise athletes that there will be adversity and unfair calls in games and that they are not a team that is so bad that they need every call to go their way to win. Championship teams practice dealing with adversity so that when it happens in a game, they are prepared and know how to react.

## CROWD NOISE AND MUSIC

An interesting technique that some college football teams use to get their team ready for the loud and crazy environment in which they often play is to have a tape of crowd noise play over the loud speaker in practice. Utilizing crowd noise or music can be effective in allowing players to practice dealing with a "hostile" environment, or an environment in which it is difficult to communicate verbally. Crowd noise provides an excellent opportunity to practice working on non-verbal methods of communication from the coaching staff to the players on the field.

The use of classical or very soft music can often make a person feel mellow or sleepy. We will play this music during practice and use it as a distraction for our players to learn to deal with. They will sometimes say, "How can you expect me to focus during practice when you are playing Beethoven?" My response is usually, "I expect you to respond the same focused way when we are in a dog fight, it is 100 degrees outside, you are dehydrated, tired and want to quit, and the same way I expect you to focus when it is raining and you are called on to pinch hit after sitting all day. I expect you to take responsibility for your thoughts, focus, and attention, by using the 30-second drill to help you force yourself to act different from how you feel."

## COMPETITIVE CONDITIONING

When it comes to conditioning, many athletes are turned off by having to run long distances, foul pole to foul pole, or around the warning track. The monotony of many types of conditioning can lead an athlete to give less than their best effort and to not physiologically improve as much as they could. When conditioning, coaches should try to make conditioning as competitive as possible for the athletes or measure their progress so they can see how their effort and performance matched up with what they gave on their best day.

One simple drill for baseball players that increases the intensity of conditioning, while having fun, is running football patterns. Something as simple as pass patterns and trying to catch a ball makes conditioning and running sprints more fun. Something else to consider with conditioning is that measurement equals motivation. This means when performance is timed, counted or measured, coaches and athletes can evaluate progress and reward extraordinary efforts. Rewarded behaviors are repeated behaviors and by structuring competitive conditioning sessions coaches can get more out of the time they've invested.

## MOTOR LEARNING MEETS BASEBALL

Scientific research in the area of motor learning and skill acquisition has demonstrated that there are three types of practice -- blocked, random, and variable that yield different and sometimes misleading results. Blocked practice is executing the same skill for a given number of times in succession. For example, a pitcher in the preseason working on location, throwing 30 fastballs to the right side of the plate, then 30 fastballs to the left side of the plate, typically finds short term success and an increase in confidence but not much longer in the way of term retention or application to game conditions. The pitcher will do well hitting spots during his 30 warm-up pitches, but when he gets in a game-like situation and has to move the ball around with each pitch, he will experience less control than during the blocked practice.

Variable practice sessions have the pitcher throwing five pitches to the left side, then five pitches to the right side, repeating this process until he has thrown 60 pitches. Variable practice will lead to less immediate success and, subsequently, less immediate confidence than the athletes who are practicing in a blocked manner. However, the athlete who trains in a variable manner will be more successful at long-term retention and will be performing the skill in a more game like situation than the person who practices in a blocked practice setting.

The best type of practice to achieve game success is random practice. Random practice entails the pitcher throwing 60 pitches in a completely random order, preferably called by the catcher. Random practice has been documented as the least effective in immediate success, but most effective in retention and long-term performance. The use of blocked, variable or random practice depends on whether the coach's goal for practice is confidence building, short-term success or long-term success.

Batting practice is a classic example of blocked practice in which the pitcher consistently throws 4-seam fastballs over the center of the plate. Batting practice of this manner is less effective for game like simulation practice where the hitter has specific situations in which they are trying to execute. Rarely does a pitcher throw in the same location with the same pitch at the same speed on successive pitches. However, one of the goals of batting practice is to increase a hitter's confidence and one of the best ways to do that for short term success is through blocked practice.

## JOLLY RANCHER PLAYER OF THE DAY

A fun technique that is used to help increase player motivation is the Jolly Rancher Player of The Day Award. After practice or a game, the coaches will decide on a player who they feel is deserving of the Jolly Rancher Player of the Day Award and will announce it in front of the team at the end of the practice or game. The Player of the Day Award is based on hustle, attitude, effort and performance or something specific for that day such as being a great team player.

The player of the practice is equally if not more important than the player of the game because there is more practice time than game time during a season. If the player is putting in the quality practice necessary to be awarded the practice player of the day, they are giving themselves the best chance for success come game time. Coaches tally the number of awards, and at the end-of-the-year banquet give out a Jolly Rancher Player of The Year Award.

## BLUE ANGEL DEBRIEFING

Perhaps equally important as pre-practice planning is post-practice debriefing. After the U.S. Navy Blue Angel Pilots fly an exhibition show, they will spend two or three times as long debriefing than it took them to fly the show. They critique everything from the way they marched to the plane, to looking at high-speed videotape of the aerial maneuvers performed.

Coaches have to continue to get better. One of the ways to do this is by debriefing after each practice session. Coaches should ask the players and other coaches, "What did we learn today and what can we do better tomorrow?" The staff will then go over the practice plan and change any details that they believed can make practice run more smoothly. They will also assess and discuss individual and team performance. From that evaluation, they decide on what to focus on in the next practice session.

The above-mentioned practice techniques have been successful with various programs that I have worked with. If you have any techniques you use to increase the quality of your practice, please email your ideas to *brian@briancain. com* for future editions of this book.

O lympic athletes, professional golfers, mixed martial arts fighting World Champions and Major League baseball players have all reported successfully using mental imagery as part of their conditioning and preparation programs. Unfortunately, many college and high school programs have not developed a similar approach to maximizing the mental game through mental imagery.

Often left out of the preparation process, mental imagery, also known as visualization and mental rehearsal, is one of the most important skills an athlete can utilize to help perform at the highest possible level on a consistent basis. Let's explore the benefits of mental imagery and take a look at how a coach or player can start a mental imagery program.

## IMAGINATION IS REALITY

There is plenty of research in sports psychology that demonstrates the benefits of mental imagery. The main reason why mental imagery helps performance is that the brain processes both vividly imagined information and physically experienced information in similar ways within the same psychoneuromuscular pathways. What happens when we do mental rehearsal is that we are conditioning our bodies to practice executing the imagined processes we formulate in our minds.

If I were to ask any randomly selected person to close his eyes and grab a lemon wedge off the counter, raise it to his lips, and take a big bite, he would probably start to have a physiological response to this psychological stimulus; similarly, if a person has seen a scary movie and literally jumped out of her seat, she has experienced a physiological response to again, a psychological stimulus; and if someone has déjà vu, he too has experienced a physiological response to a psychological stimulus -- exactly the same type of response he would get from engaging in mental imagery.

In athletics, the preparation process is similar for every sport in that any athlete will benefit greatly from consistently practicing mental imagery, which is to say that a player will improve significantly if she practices imagining herself playing at her best, being aggressive and playing with a relaxed intensity. Mentally reliving past best performances also increases the chances of repeating them exactly as they happened before.

I remember a player recalling an "at-bat" he had earlier this season against Mississppi State where we had done some mental rehearsal in the hotel before the game in which he saw himself driving an inside fastball over the shortstop's head for an RBI single. In the game later that night, the same scenario came up and played out exactly as he had seen it in his mind earlier that day. It was a pretty cool experience for that player who stood on first base, looked in the dugout and laughed like he had planned it to happen that way.

## UTILIZE AS MANY SENSES AS POSSIBLE
One of the Mixed Martial Arts Fighting World Champions I have worked with told me "There is a big difference between doing mental imagery and just thinking about the fight." This is true in other sports as well. Often players and coaches can confuse thinking about the game

with practicing mental imagery. One difference is that mental imagery involves a good deal more deliberate effort and time, whereas just thinking about an athletic performance is frequently shorter and not as focused. Another difference is that mental imagery is far more richly detailed, involving far more stages and images.

Along these lines, part of what makes mental imagery different from just thinking about the game and much more beneficial is that it builds upon more sensory feedback. For example, if an athlete is mentally rehearsing offensive scenarios, he will want to be sure he includes the color of the uniform the pitcher is wearing and the background he would see behind the pitcher. In addition, he should imagine the release point, the ball, contact with the pitch and the ball rocketing off of his bat barrel. He would then want to see himself making contact on the inside corner of first base with his right foot as he explodes in a desperate sprint to second base, beating the throw with a good aggressive popup slide.

He would then want to build in the sense of sound and hear the ball hit the bat, hear his body slide aggressively into second base, and hear the positive energy coming from the dugout and the crowd. Additionally, he would also want to build in the sense of smell and touch by feeling the ball make contact with the bat and smell the warm spring day, the smell of freshly cut grass and the barbeque behind the stadium. Building-in as many senses as possible will help him to make the imagery experience more real and beneficial.

## CREATING A STAGE FOR SUCCESS

Ideally, to engage in the mental imagery exercise, athletes should begin rehearsing in a quiet and controlled environment by eliminating all distractions so they will not be disturbed and can totally focus on the task at hand. As they become more experienced, confident and clear with their imagery, they should start to build in distractions such as a cell phone ringing, crowd noise playing from a CD, or the lights in the room flickering on and off so that they can learn how to stay focused and on task.

This kind of exercise can be compared to an athlete learning to deal with the distractions and pressures of playing in front of a hostile crowd in a championship game where there are many intense distractions for him to deal with. Athletes and coaches can easily be derailed by distractions not relevant to their staying focused on the task at hand, so it is of utmost importance that they prepare themselves for this certain eventuality.

## USING IMAGERY WHEN RECOVERING FROM INJURY

Having been a pitcher in college who spent the majority of his time in the training room and on the disabled list, I have found that utilizing mental rehearsal with athletes who are injured has tremendous benefits. When you are injured and can't compete, often you get labeled with a red X, sit on the sidelines, watch practice feeling sorry for yourself, and waste time you could be spending on mental imagery.

One athlete that made the most of his time on the disabled list ended up being a first round draft pick and was one of the best hitters in college baseball history. This player broke his hand in the first game of the 2008 season, and with the help of his coaching staff and athletic trainer, he was able to stay sharp by taking mental at-bats during games and when standing in for pitchers who were throwing in the bullpen. Here is what he said:

> I wasn't able to swing, but I was able to hold a bat. I would go to the bullpen and stand in when guys were pitching so I could track the ball and do as much physically as I could. I would then step out of the batter's box, take a full swing in my mind and see myself making solid contact. I would see the same pitch, see myself taking a healthy cut at it, hear the solid contact and then see the ball fly out of the park. I would also do some one-handed bunting, visualize my base running by getting good reads off the crack of the bat and really working hard to field the ball defensively.
>
> During games, I would visualize myself at the plate going pitch for pitch with the guy who was hitting in my spot in the line up. I would grab my bat, helmet and batting gloves each time that spot came up in the line up and would take a mental at-bat right there in the dugout.
>
> When my hand finally healed and I was cleared to swing a bat again, I felt like a lot of the rust most people experience coming off of an injury was already gone. I was truly surprised at how I was able to pick up where I had left off. Taking all of that mental practice really helped me stay in the flow of the game so that I could make a successful comeback in the least amount of time.

## MENTAL IMAGERY OF GAME SITUATIONS

Below is a sample list of game situations that can be used to conduct mental imagery sessions. It is important to build in as many of the senses as possible – sight, sound, smell, touch, taste. Both right and left handed pitching should also be considered when dealing with this list.

- Fastball away, driven into the opposite field gap with a hard pop up slide into second base
- Fastball in, pulled down the line
- Runner at first base, moved to third with a base hit to the right side of the field
- Sacrifice bunt with runners on first and second base
- Suicide squeeze bunt down in fair territory
- Hit and run with a runner at first base
- With a runner at third base, the is ball driven towards the middle of the infield to score the runner
- You are the base runner at first base, advance to second base with a breaking ball down in the dirt
- You are the runner on second base, score on a base hit through the infield sliding hard into home plate
- Batter gets base hit into left field through the gap between the short stop and third basemen, runs hard the entire way non-stop, aggressively round first base to put pressure on the left fielder to make a good throw to second base while he continues on to second base and beats the throw

With mental imagery, athletes can create any situation they want to prepare for. The more detailed the scenario, the more beneficial the imagery session will be. Players can see the coach giving signs from the third base coaching box; players can mentally rehearse going through their hitting routines and releasing their red lights; furthermore adversity can be built in such as an umpire making a bad call on a fastball down the middle that should have been called as a strike but instead was called as a ball.

By conditioning players to see processes and outcomes in their minds and getting them to experience the kind of responses they would like to experience in a game, players will have a better chance of getting desired outcomes to happen as they have envisioned them happening on the field in their mind before the game ever starts.

*If you are interested in having Brian Cain create a custom mental imagery audio for you or your team, please visit our contact us page at www.briancain.com and send Cain a message that you are interested in having him create a custom mental imagery program for you or your team.*

Visit www.ToiletsBricksFishHooksAndPride.com
For FREE Extras, Updates & Information

# CHAPTER 10 | WHAT'S YOUR ROLE ON THIS TEAM?

Eagle or Duck? Fountain or Drain?
Bent Nickel or War Dog?

### DISCUSSING PLAYER ROLES

Most of the coaches and athletes I work with at the high school and college level agree that clear and frequent communication between the coach and player is essential for understanding and acceptance of roles. One way to improve communication with players is to discuss the finer details of the role(s) they may play this season.

Role clarification can help an athlete better understand a coach's expectations, can be used as a motivational tool, and unfortunately can also box players in and make them feel like no matter how hard they work or how much they improve, they are only going to be second string, a bench player or bullpen catcher unless a clearly communicated path is defined for them to fulfill their expectations.

## OPEN-ENDED DISCUSSION OF ROLES ESSENTIAL

It is important that coaches expect and communicate to their athletes the importance of going all out every day and play to the best of their ability one day at a time. By doing this, they give themselves the best chance for skill improvement, role improvement and end result success.

## EAGLES AND DUCKS

Every team has members who are ducks or eagles. Ducks are the team members that whine, complain and quack about their situation -- the players that think blowing out someone else's candle makes theirs burn brighter. Ducks are the athletes that want the person playing in front of them to get injured so that they can crack the line-up. They quack about people behind their back and will never be counted on as a great teammate. This is an immature and unfortunate situation that I see all too often in high school, collegiate, and especially professional sports.

Eagles, on the other hand, soar above. They may not like their situation on the team, but they choose to keep their mouths shut and work until their situation improves. They do not participate in the back-stabbing or locker room lobbying that happens in too many programs. Champions choose a higher road and try to be team builders and confidence creators rather than team breakers and confidence destroyers.

## FOUNTAINS AND DRAINS

Much like the duck, the drain is an energy dissipater. The drain sucks out the energy and enthusiasm people bring to the party with their destructive tactics. When they make mistakes, they do not go down alone and often look for other people that they can pull down with them. Drains have a negative effect on other players and teams. They will suck the life out of players and crush their season.

Fountains are the energy providers. They work to pump up their teammates and carry themselves with a positive energy and attitude regardless of the situation. Fountains may not have their best game that day but are always considered the best teammates to have because they will always be there to help everyone else and celebrate their teammates' success.

## BENT NICKELS

For a great visual demonstration to the team about roles and the importance of communicating well, take a roll of nickels, bend a few of the nickels into a V-shape using two pairs of pliers, then stack them up on top of each other. If the nickels being stacked are perfectly formed, undistorted well-rounded nickels, they will be able to be stacked up high, perhaps higher than expected. If, on the other hand, there is a bent nickel in the center or on the bottom as the foundation, the stack of nickels will collapse instead of standing tall.

A tall stack of nickels, of course, is a metaphor for an athletic team or any kind of group that depends upon teamwork. Teams are very interdependent on the skills, motivation, preparation, talent, clear communications and many other elements possessed by the team members and coach. Some teammates may be able to be stacked on top of other distorted, flawed teammates, but not many. For a stack to be piled high, it must be resting on a strong core, well formed foundation with no bent nickels.

**WAR DOGS – THE BEST COMPLIMENT A COACH CAN GIVE**
Winning on the scoreboard is a by-product of many
things. One critical piece is having everyone giving
100% of themselves to fulfilling their role on the team.
Unfortunately, bench players often complain about
a lack of playing time, second-class status, and never
completely embrace and accept their role as critically
important backup and specialty players on the team –
what is sometimes referred to as bench strength. Too
many are discouraged and depressed energy ducks and
drains. One of the best ways to motivate bench players is
to challenge them to be war dogs.

Since ancient time, dogs have been trained as a valuable weapon for times of war. A war dog is a dog trained specifically for the combat and conflict met on the battle field. Their jobs have varied over the years, from being trained to diffuse mines with their acute sense of smell to sensing trouble nearby with their acute sense of hearing to bringing down infantry or even horses by biting into the hamstrings of their targets. Sometimes these war dogs will even step on a mine or get in the way of enemy fire to save a soldier, giving their lives for the betterment of the team.

In athletics the term war dog is used to describe the player that says something like, "...Yes coach I will do whatever you ask me to do to help the team get better. If you want me to throw at batting practice, I will be the best batting practice pitcher in the nation; and if you want me to pick up sunflower seeds in the cage, I can do that too. I can do anything that you think will help us get better as a team and give ourselves the best chance to win..."

War dogs can be the players who are the glue that holds the team together. Before selecting a war dog, a war dog candidate should listen to a thorough explanation about the importance of the role, the history and significance of the position, the necessity of having a selfless attitude, the positive impact a war dog can have on a team, the value of the charts being kept by the war dog, the ready reserve position war dogs hold to step in for any team member at a moment's notice, and the jobs war dogs do to propel team success. These are all things that can help keep a student athlete who might otherwise become a duck or a drain from going down that path.

Whatever is done, be careful who is called a war dog. Being a war dog is a privilege and an honor only bestowed upon a few. The war dog plaque that hangs in your office will be graced with the names of the greatest teammates in program history, people that are truly selfless and people that will eventually become great coaches. To be called a war dog can become the greatest honor anyone can earn in your program. Use the term sparingly and select only a few for the honor.

Visit www.ToiletsBricksFishHooksAndPride.com
For FREE Extras, Updates & Information

## Only One Way of Getting Up To Speed

For years sport psychologists and peak performance coaches have used the concentration grid to help athletes train their abilities to concentrate and focus on the present moment. Success in athletics has nothing to do with magic dust or hocus-pocus. It has everything to do with the ability to focus and, when that ability is inevitably distracted, refocus on what's important now.

Michael Farber wrote an article titled *Second To One* featured in the April 16, 2007 issue of Sports Illustrated in which he discussed how Major League Baseball pitching phenom Roy Halladay uses the concentration grids as a part of his preparation for pitching. The article mentioned how Halladay completes the grid twice on the day before he starts and once more on the day that he pitches.

Many of the athletes that I work with at the collegiate and professional level use concentration grids as a way to focus in the present moment for an extended period of time. The purpose of the exercise is to narrow the focus and quiet the mind into the present moment focused on only the next number. We talk a lot about playing the game one pitch, one play, one shift, or one possession at a time. The concentration grid is designed to help an athlete work one number at a time. Much like athletes want the ability to relax and manage their mental and emotional states when the game is on the line, the concentration grid enables them to start being able to control mental and emotional states in a quiet and calm environment.

When Halladay began working the concentration grid (a 10-square-by-10-square grid), he needed 17 to 20 minutes to finish the exercise. Now he has become so proficient that his average time is about three and a half minutes. In addition, he doesn't need absolute quiet any more as he did when he started. He can amp up the distractions with TV or music and still function perfectly.

Living by the concept that measurement equals motivation, I started working with the concentration grid more frequently, doing it a-little-a-lot vs. a-lot-a-little, if you catch my drift. I would do one before breakfast every Monday, Wednesday and Friday instead of doing three or four on a Saturday. When I first started, it took me close to fifteen minutes to complete the grid. Three years later, my average time is four and a half minutes and my personal best is three and a half minutes.

Athletes I have worked with report that the grid allows them to become more aware of when their minds drift from the present moment and they lose their focus of the next number that's important now. They report that the "C-GRID" also allows them to become more aware of when they are trying too hard and need to take a breath in order to relax and get back into an optimal level of focus.

Starting the C-GRID exercise for the first time should be in a quiet, controlled environment. Quiet means no cell phone, no TV and no other distractions. The quiet, controlled environment enhances the development of a heightened awareness of what is going on, including the possibility of being distracted by other thoughts.

After gaining some experience with the C-GRID exercise, turning on the TV or music and gradually increasing the volume over time while continuing the exercise on, will provide valuable experience in handling distractions. Mastery of mind over matter won't happen instantaneously. Ideally what should happen is awareness of the distraction will trigger refocusing on the next number so that the TV and music fades into the background and the exercise proceeds in the moment.

In addition to a quiet, controlled environment to do the exercise, you will need a C-GRID, a timer, and a black marker or pen. Sample C-GRIDs are found below. An unlimited variety of C-GRIDs can be purchased at *www. briancain.com*. The marker should be used to completely cross out the numbers in sequence starting with 00 and working to 99 as quickly as possible. With the C-GRID face down, start the timer, then turn over the C-GRID and keep track of the time. If using a marker, the number should be crossed out completely, time to complete the exercise will shorten because the numbers crossed out can't be seen. Using a pencil will enable the numbers to be read, increasing the time needed to finish.

I have used this exercise with elementary school students and Olympic athletes. All have reported the ability to recognize when they get distracted and to improve their abilities to pull their focus back into the present moment. Have fun with the C-GRID. Compete against your best time and feel yourself increase your ability to focus in the present moment.

## Brian Cain Peak Performance, LLC

www.BrianCain.com
www.BrianCainInnerCircle.com
www.ToiletsBricksFishHooksAndPride.com
www.SoWhatNextPitch.com
www.MentalConditioningManual.com

| 39 | 48 | 59 | 28 | 71 | 26 | 34 | 70 | 95 | 06 |
|----|----|----|----|----|----|----|----|----|----|
| 21 | 91 | 42 | 12 | 30 | 84 | 76 | 97 | 61 | 75 |
| 58 | 08 | 85 | 32 | 45 | 66 | 36 | 63 | 23 | 29 |
| 96 | 80 | 00 | 88 | 89 | 11 | 25 | 57 | 02 | 90 |
| 74 | 33 | 56 | 93 | 52 | 73 | 04 | 10 | 49 | 19 |
| 87 | 09 | 16 | 81 | 69 | 38 | 64 | 50 | 83 | 41 |
| 31 | 01 | 40 | 47 | 18 | 77 | 24 | 14 | 13 | 60 |
| 79 | 72 | 05 | 51 | 82 | 55 | 15 | 17 | 44 | 94 |
| 54 | 35 | 53 | 68 | 65 | 20 | 03 | 99 | 86 | 27 |
| 67 | 46 | 07 | 78 | 22 | 92 | 37 | 62 | 98 | 43 |

## Brian Cain Peak Performance, LLC

www.BrianCain.com
www.BrianCainInnerCircle.com
www.ToiletsBricksFishHooksAndPride.com
www.SoWhatNextPitch.com
www.MentalConditioningManual.com

| 39 | 48 | 59 | 28 | 71 | 26 | 34 | 70 | 95 | 06 |
|----|----|----|----|----|----|----|----|----|----|
| 21 | 91 | 42 | 12 | 30 | 84 | 76 | 97 | 61 | 75 |
| 58 | 08 | 85 | 32 | 45 | 66 | 36 | 63 | 23 | 29 |
| 96 | 80 | 00 | 88 | 89 | 11 | 25 | 57 | 02 | 90 |
| 74 | 33 | 56 | 93 | 52 | 73 | 04 | 10 | 49 | 19 |
| 87 | 09 | 16 | 81 | 69 | 38 | 64 | 50 | 83 | 41 |
| 31 | 01 | 40 | 47 | 18 | 77 | 24 | 14 | 13 | 60 |
| 79 | 72 | 05 | 51 | 82 | 55 | 15 | 17 | 44 | 94 |
| 54 | 35 | 53 | 68 | 65 | 20 | 03 | 99 | 86 | 27 |

# PART II

## Championship Coaches Share How They Maximize The Mental Game

# CHAPTER 12 | EATING THE MENTAL GAME FOR BREAKFAST

The Real Breakfast of Champions

Reading Memorial High School Baseball Coach Peter Moscariello has been the school's skipper since 1977. One of the most successful coaches in Massachusetts, Moscariello has learned that it is not necessarily the best team that always wins; rather, it is more often the team that plays the best that goes home victorious.

Moscariello, like many coaches, started off his career by immersing himself in the x's and o's of baseball, but has since come to the realization that the mental game is as critical to championship baseball as any other component. This is what he has described when asked about it:

> In the mid-90s, we had some great teams and that was when we introduced our players to *The Mental Game of Baseball* by Dorfman. We would go over chapters and talk about the material, but I never really felt our players were able to grasp and apply the information as well as we wanted them to. A few years ago, when I saw some articles on mental toughness Cain had written, I purchased some of his DVDs, and the Mental Game really came to life for me because I was able to see the material being applied in real game situations.

## CLASSROOM SESSION A SUCCESS

Moscariello holds regular classroom sessions for his players on the mental game. Since he deals with time limitations, he has to be efficient with his use of time by getting his players centered and focused to enable a quality session.

I have found that when we can show our players a visual that they are able to understand and discuss, they will apply the principles a lot more rapidly and consistently than if we just give them something to read. When we take this approach, we are able to take it to another level. We have been so impressed with the results of this program that what Cain calls 'The Mental Game' is now a part of what we do every day. Whether it's watching one of Cain's PRIDE DVDs, listening to one of his CDs, or sharing a *One Minute Motivation* lesson, our athletes have really bought into the concepts of peak performance, self-control and focusing on the process over the end result.

We've integrated these valuable teaching materials directly into our coaching process. We usually start by meeting 10-12 weeks before the particular athletic season we are engaged in begins. We invite as many people as we can persuade from other groups and from our own program to watch the DVDs as a group in the same sitting. Following that, we have group discussions about the content. After that, we usually have each of our players individually research and write up a topic such as imagining situational challenges, constructing confidence or practicing performance routines.

Finally, each athlete on our team presents how the various mental procedures they've done research on can help them enhance performance when it means the most.

I'm very pleased with this approach because it has given our athletes ownership of the material that, in turn has propelled their development faster and further.

We are at the point where our athletes have internalized the mental game approach. Specifically, they are really applying the information we talk about in the classroom to the field. A great example of this is they have really bought into and are applying the K minus A = Zero principal, which translated means knowledge without action is useless.

## MENTAL GAME MEETS MATH CLASS

Moscariello is a math teacher as well as a baseball coach. He decided to bring some of the mental game skills he was experiencing success with on the diamond into the classroom to try to increase the motivation and enhance the learning experience of his students. Here's what he described.

> I was so impressed with the effect that Brian Cain's mental toughness program had on our baseball players that I decided to experiment to see if the mental skills I was teaching in baseball would also help them in the math classes I teach and in life as well.

I introduced them to the Cain concept of how signal lights impacted them in the classroom and in life. It's a simple concept. Green means things are going well and red, not so well. The kids caught on quickly. The hard part is awareness of which signal light you are in and being able to go from red to green as quickly as possible. I then told them about another Cain concept illustrated by the story of the donkey who fell into the well and needed to shake it off and step up. Here was a donkey who when stuck in a well and thought the dirt thrown down in the well was meant to bury him, until he changed his point of view and realized that it was a means of escape by just shaking off whatever landed on him and stepping up on top of the dirt. I then followed up with a discussion about how those concepts related to their everyday lives and the ensuing discussions were amazing. They talked about things they have experienced in work, with their families and in other parts of their lives. It was eye opening for me to hear them talk about things going on in their lives.

I think that for most students, motivation to do your best was a mystery beyond their power to do anything about. I introduced this subject by asking the students as they entered my classroom how they felt (in general) on a scale of 1 to 10 with 10 being the best and 1 being the worst. In response, some would say they felt like a two and others would say they felt like a five. After everyone had offered up their number, we would have a class discussion about how emotions can be changed by motions and similarly, how proactive actions, positive responses and self-talk (as distinguished from impulsive reactions) can change attitudes. After our discussion, I gave them an assignment to walk in and just say they felt like a 10 no matter how they really felt. So they all did. Then we waited to see what would happen.

While we were waiting, I decided to enrich the discussion and fill in the blanks, so to speak about the faking it till you make it, million-dollar mentality point-of-view. I told them that if they could start to give a 10 effort in everything they did, especially when they did not feel like it, by faking it, that it would not be long before they would have their pick of million dollar jobs. The rationale I gave them was that in life, as in baseball, it's truly a matter of will over skill and energetic effort over ability. We can't control everything, but we can control what goes on in our minds and how much effort we give.

Along with giving my students the rationale for faking it, we also talked a lot about the Brian Cain pointer of being right here, right now in the present moment and controlling the controllable. The broader view of being in the present is about awareness of what needs doing and awareness of the direction you're headed in. It's not a good idea to escape from the present for long.

Good posture, relaxed body language, firm hand shakes and maintenance of strong eye contact has also been the subject of repeated conversations I've had with the students. These are all related elements of the faking it follow-through. If the students aren't doing this, their faking will not be credible.

I've used the 30-second drill when I've needed to make a critical teaching point to lock in and focus my athletes. Sometimes we do this for our full 90 minute classes, 30 seconds at a time. While in other conversations I've helped my athletes identify then leave outside the door the mental bricks they may be carrying around with them as well as all of their other negatives.

This may sound strange, but ever since we started on this new focus on mental toughness, my students and I have used math class as a respite from math. The subject reversal has been a lot of fun. I've been able to hold their attention better, present math concepts in a more receptive atmosphere and have better relationships with my students outside of class than ever before. Astonishingly, to top that all off, everyone's grades have improved.

We also write positive affirmations or confidence conditioning statements on the board before a test just as I would before a baseball game. I would write, 'I know the material, I can do this and I am good at math' on the board and the students have said, 'Wow, I really like that stuff because I find myself saying it in my head during the test and I find that it helps me to be more confident and relaxed during the test.'

What is so surprising is that the students have been more positive, more upbeat and are performing better than any class at this level that I have ever had. I would highly encourage coaches who are also teachers to try some of these things in their classroom along with what they are doing with their teams. I think it has helped me to be more motivated and to be a better teacher and coach than I have ever been.

It has made a huge impact on the quality of our classes and on their interest in coming to class.

## MAXIMIZING INDOOR PRACTICE

Playing high school baseball in Massachusetts often means contending with cold, wet weather. In such a climate, indoor practice, though not ideal, can be a recipe for going through the motions. Moscariello found that spending time on mental training – the kind of training that doesn't depend upon good weather, has paid dividends in improving the attention and focus of his athletes.

Each time we start a drill our hitters go through a routine, we have them look at the label on the bat, take a good deep breath, touch the corner of the plate and get locked in with their swing thought, the last conscious thought before the pitcher throws focused on having quality game-like repetitions.

Every time we hit live in the indoor batting cage it is a game-like situation where we record results. We've found that our high school-aged athletes stay motivated and continue to work hard when practicing indoors when we make drills competitive and game-like. Measuring results such as strike outs, walks and hits is done in real game settings so that's what we do in practice. We buy into the concept that measurement equals motivation, so we carry this right down to the smallest detail. For example, we have our team members go through a post-practice or post-game release routine in which players review all the actions they've taken during practice or a game before taking off their uniforms and releasing their baseball personas. In addition, we also have them practice warm-up routines as would typically be done when the player is on deck and in the hole preparing for an at-bat.

We also have our pitchers go through form drills where they are working on the basics of throwing mechanics for various types of pitches without actually throwing a ball. In addition, we also have them visualize executing pitches and dealing with adversity by purposely making bad calls against them when we scrimmage or when they are practicing pitching.

## MENTAL GAME LANGUAGE TAKES OVER PROGRAM

One of the signs that your team has bought into the mental game is that they use a common language to talk about their experiences. What might sound strange to a person not a part of the program has deep meaning to those who are battling in the trenches. Many of the terms such as Crabs, APE, ACE, Green Lights, WIN, Make The Days Count, Get Big, 200 Feet and Control What You Can Control are only recognizable for people who are versed in the mental game. Moscariello has found that language has taken a life of its own in his program.

I regularly overhear this kind of special player code about their keeping the mental game sharp along with the regular playing chatter people are used to in baseball games. For example, I heard from our dugout the other day a few of the players on the bench say to one of the hitters at the plate 'So What, Next Pitch (translation: get over it, what's next)! Get Green Here' (translation: stay positive, focus on what you want to do, not what you are trying to avoid). If you aren't up on this kind of talk, you wouldn't know what was going on. It's amazing how this kind of verbalizing has escalated. These days, our players are always talking about winning this inning, winning this pitch, or winning this swing. They have really internalized the approach to focus on mastering each small step in the process instead of worrying about the outcome.

Our locker room is plastered with signs that remind us of the Mental Game language such as GET BIG,

WIN (What's Important Now), Confidence Is A Choice, and Control the Controllable. It serves as a constant reminder for everyone in the program. I think last year they did a lot of these things because they thought that it was what I or the other coaches wanted them to do, but now they have taken ownership and it is a part of who they are and what they do.

## PLAYERS EXPERIENCE SUCCESS

When players start to work on their mental game, they have to realize that the mental game is comprised of a set of mental skills that need to be developed over a period of time through constant training and conditioning, similar to the way they train and condition their bodies to execute physical skills. When players accept that mental skills produce desired results on the scoreboard and do the skill building work, they increase their chances at having more successful results.

Practicing mental skills requires a different, more immediate way of thinking where players are more focused on the process instead of the end result. Most players really adjust quite easily to this approach and you can see this clearly in their commentary and performance. When asked, most players say they are less pressured, more relaxed, more confident and more focused on the process than the end result. That helps to take the pressure off and enables them to relax, which in turn leads to better performance. For example, if their goal is to see the ball big and have a quality swing, this approach will lead to quality contact that leads to a quality at-bat which, in turn, may lead to a quality result. In the larger picture, they understand that baseball is a game of averages where averages improve when processes improve. Immediate results can come from the interaction of many factors, many of which are not controllable. Worrying about the uncontrollable is not a productive use of time.

Our players have made the transformation from working hard to working smart. They have gone from trying to get as many repetitions and as many swings as they can to getting quality game-like repetitions, focusing on the quality, not quantity. Don't get me wrong, we still drill them on the mechanics of how to swing, how to field and how to pitch, but we spend more time than ever talking about the process of playing and their mental approach.

## POST-PERFORMANCE EVALUATION CRITICAL
After each game and before his players take off their uniforms and 'release' being a baseball player, Moscariello asks them to: visualize each of their at-bats, evaluate their performance and imagine their future efforts at achieving excellence.

We have them evaluate their individual performance after each game on a few simple criteria that they have complete control over.

1. Was I in control of myself?
2. Did I see the ball well?
3. Did I get a good swing?
4. Did I make good contact?

They have to learn where it didn't work out for them to improve. We call it 'locating the black box.'

For example, if the at-bat fell apart because the player was not in control of himself, then that is what he needs to work on. If it was not seeing the ball, than the player needs to spend more time training the eyes and tracking. What the post-game evaluation lets us find out is what we need to improve upon as a part of the process to perform better. We have become a program that strives for excellence as distinguished from a program that strives to win. Winning is a byproduct of doing the little things the right way on a daily basis. Winning is a byproduct of striving for excellence. Excellence is not necessarily a byproduct of winning.

# CHAPTER 13 | A BOOTCAMP OBSTACLE COURSE LOADED WITH FISH HOOKS

## How to Get Off The Gaff

Rick Lynch, the head baseball coach at Tomball High School in Tomball, Texas was the 2004 Louisville Slugger National High School Coach of The Year. Lynch took an interesting approach to preparing his team for the 2008 season. Already having one of the premiere high school baseball programs in the nation, Lynch knew that if he was going to prepare his team to play championship caliber baseball, it was going to be done with a one-pitch-at-a-time mentality, attention to detail, and a don't-count-the-days, make-the-days-count attitude. Lynch shared some of the interesting techniques he used to prepare his teams to get the most out of every day.

### OBSTACLE COURSE WARM UP ROUTINE

Having one of the only programs in the nation that uses an extensive obstacle course during pre-game warm-ups both at home and on the road, Lynch had to first convince his players that stepping outside of the box (bucking the norm) was the best approach and would give his team a competitive advantage.

Dennis Faye and Ron Wolforth introduced me to the rugby stretch and dynamic warm-up procedures they use. This warm up is now a cornerstone in our program at Tomball. I think the final acceptance of this direction by the team happened when we invited

Nike SPARQ this fall to evaluate our athletes and SPARQ put them through a similar warm-up like the one we had been doing already.

Our athletes have really embraced the approach and now are enthusiastic about doing warm-ups. Often the other team will be looking over at us watching what we are doing, rather than focusing on their own warm-up. The use of the dynamic warm-up allows our players to get loose, break a sweat, and get physically and mentally prepared while having fun.

## FISHING ANALOGY CATCHES ON

Lynch and his assistants Rusty Reeder and Kirk Youngdale were looking for a team building activity that they could use to break up the monotony of the pre-season and decided that a catfish hunting experience was the best medicine.

One day, coming home from a game where we did not play well, we asked our bus driver to pull over by a roadside fishing spot. As we prepared to stop, many of the players looked confused and one even asked if we were going to do laps as a form of punishment? "No," I shot back with a grin ear to ear. "We're going to flush the game and go fishing." Instantly the team's obvious tension turned to smiles, laughter and excited chatter all around; and at the end of the day, after a really great afternoon blowing off steam, everyone agreed that the fishing trip was one of the best things we've ever done as a team. As a result, we came up with the slogan -- "Don't Get Hooked" to remind our players of all the outside circumstances that can hinder their performance – the fans, the weather, the other team, the umpire, the professional draft, and all the other things that they can't control. Instead, we emphasized that they should focus on things that they can control such as playing the game one pitch at a time.

This kind of ability to remain in control is everything in baseball. We've encouraged our players to stay away from the "baited hooks in the water" – small distractions waiting to lure a purposeless player to an unsatisfactory end. The baseball player that can focus on what he wants and ignore the things he can't control is able to get on with the next pitch and much of the time, a successful outcome.

## W.I.N. THIS PITCH – KEEP YOUR MIND IN THE MOMENT
Lynch and his staff have developed a language with their players that they constantly use to keep the team positive and focused on the present moment.

'Win this at-bat' , 'flush it', 'zone in zone out,' 'stay big,' 'your best game now,' and 'W.I.N.', are all things that our athletes and coaches say on a routine basis. The term W.I.N. means to focus on **W**hat's **I**mportant **N**ow. To WIN this pitch, an athlete must be collectively more focused on this pitch than his opponents.

Our players understand that when the ball leaves their hand, or their bat, they no longer have any control over what happens. A good pitch or bad pitch, good hit or bad hit, we play the game one pitch at a time, no matter the result. It's always about the next pitch.

## ROUTINES HELP PLAYERS REACH THEIR POTENTIAL

Lynch and the Tomball staff work individually with each player to develop a routine to help keep the players positive and focused on each pitch. Here's what Lynch has said:

> Understanding the mental rehearsal routine and how to breathe helps athletes to focus and play pitch by pitch. We also spend a lot of time talking about signal lights (red, yellow, green) and what situations cause our players to speed up their routines and get out of synch. When our players do speed up their routines, we remind our players to step off the mound or out of the batter's box and take the (fish) hook out. When players have the ability to understand inner thoughts and emotions, the player can let go of a hook they may have been snagged on and focus on their current play.

## DEALING WITH ADVERSITY

Baseball is a game of adversity and it's often the sudden adverse turn of events that lead teams into inconsistent performances. The team that is able to adapt and overcome the quickest will be the team that plays most consistently and will have the best chance to win more games.

One way to develop the ability to overcome adversity is to "throw in the monkeys" and prepare for adversity in practice. In other words, simulate any number of unexpected and usually undesired turns of events. By getting players to be comfortable with being uncomfortable and by practicing adverse situations in practice, players learn to handle the adversity that comes "unexpectedly" in games. Lynch recollected the following:

> We've used a lot of Brian Cain's DVDs to help educate our staff and players on how to be comfortable with being uncomfortable. I heard Ken Ravizza talk about how a heart surgeon must always be focused and confident during each operation, or he risks the life of his patient. It's the same in baseball. We must be confident on every pitch and every at-bat. We practice walking to the plate with confidence on a daily basis.
>
> In practice, we will intentionally 'blow' calls to test if our players will respond appropriately. This is one of the things Cain has really helped us with. He came to work with us at Tomball and ran a twelve-hour boot camp where we went back and forth from the classroom and the field with our players. It made a remarkable difference.

The other day our team was at the plate with a three and one count. An obvious ball four crosses the zone and is called a strike. Our hitter steps out of the box, clears (his mind of) the pitch by taking a deep breath and cleaning out the box with his spikes. He then gets back in the box focused and ready to go, the same way we practice every day in batting practice. You should have heard the players in the dugout get behind him in support. It was incredible. He then smacked a double off the wall in left center field. The game rewarded him for staying in control of his emotions when he could have easily been 'hooked' (disrupted, unnerved, lost his cool) by the umpire's bad call.

## TEACHING LIFE SKILLS THROUGH SPORT
Lynch has had success with integrating team building activities and teaching life skills in his sports by coaching

non-sports skills such as, self-control, responsibility and accountability. He described what this is all about this way:

> One of the best things we have been able to do is to get our players to learn and internalize something that is bigger than all of us individually. We have got them to sincerely believe that in ten years it won't matter who batted in the four hole or what the score of a specific game was but we will remember what kind of teammate Cam was, or what kind of coach Rusty was. In other words, we have really focused on building strong relationships and team synergy that are sustained beyond the immediate moment or season. This pays large dividends in overcoming everyday frustrations that will happen to any and all of us.

## ADVICE FOR YOUNG COACHES

Lynch admits that as his hair color has changed with age so have his philosophies on playing the game and coaching.

> Early in my career I was all about winning. I never quite knew how we did it. We just did somehow. There was no process involved. Eventually, I came to realize that winning was a byproduct of doing the right things, working the process, and from having quality relationships with the young men in our program.
>
> If you create a tight bond with your staff and players, and get them all to lock in to the team mission, you will be successful, regardless of what the scoreboard says. I have come to find that if you invest in relationships and the mental game, the scoreboard will often take care of itself and will reward you.

# CHAPTER 14 | IN SEASON – IN EASY

Practicing The Game Like Gaming The Practice

Ron Eastman, head baseball coach of The Woodlands High School in The Woodlands, Texas, led the Highlanders to the 2006 High School Baseball National Championship. Eastman shares some of his success strategies and things he believes are the foundation for building a championship program.

## EXCELLENCE ON AND OFF THE FIELD

Eastman knows that success is not like a light switch. Success cannot be turned on and off. Success is a lifestyle, not an event -- a lifestyle created by doing things the right way all of the time.

> We strive for excellence both on and off the field. I think that if the young people we serve are striving to be the best they can be in the classroom, out in the community and on the baseball field, that process does wonders for them and for the program. As staff, we are very interested in their character development and in training them to have successful futures on and off the field.

> Baseball is a great life lesson in and of itself. There is failure built into this game just about everywhere you look. I stress to them that the game of baseball is tough just as the game of life is tough. You are going to strikeout, make errors and give up homeruns both on and off the field. How you respond to that adversity is what will determine how successful you are going to be.

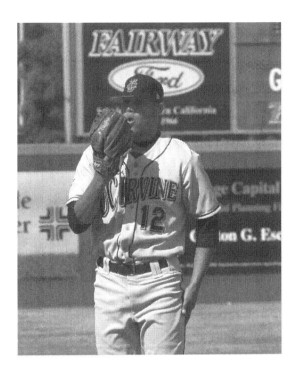

**TEACHING HOW TO RESPOND IN THE FACE OF ADVERSITY IS ESSENTIAL**

Coaches often overlook the value of teaching their players how to respond to failure. We often forget that overcoming adversity is a skill that can be learned just like hitting and throwing. We are not born with the ability to hit and we are not born with the ability to overcome adversity. We need to be taught those skills. Eastman elaborated:

> We talk a lot about imagery and visualization in our coaching. At the high school level players don't have a lot of time to master the sport, so we feel that the mental aspect of the game is a very important adjunct to our coaching. Most athletes visualize themselves being successful pretty easily, but we

turn the tables on their thinking by challenging them to imagine themselves making mistakes and responding the way they want to after they make mistakes; turning lemons into lemonade, so to speak. Whether it's a hostile crowd, an umpire making questionable calls, or a personal issue, whatever it is, we want them to anticipate any of these situations happening and see themselves handling adversity in a productive way. If we don't teach them how to respond through imagery, how will they know what to do when it happens for real?

## GAME LIKE PRACTICE

Eastman scrimmages a lot more in practice than he used to because he wants to make practice more game-like so that his players can treat games more practice-like. He wants practices to be more intense so that competing becomes a part of his player's everyday mentality.

The last few years we were successful, but we didn't make it as far into the state tournament as we wanted to. Our staff got together with some of the local college coaches and picked their brains about what they thought we could do to get our players to the next level. They all said, increase the quantity and quality of your scrimmages. So we decided to take their advice. Once we got into the season, we spent a lot more time scrimmaging than doing drill work.

One of the things I do in scrimmages is intentionally disrupt a pitcher's expectations about how a game should flow. For example, I make an obviously bad call to see how a pitcher will react and respond. Kyle Drabek was one of our high profile pitchers who had taken a lot of abuse from fans who came to our games in his first few years. I think a lot of them crossed the line in what was said for a high school baseball game, but it also showed me that we needed to do a better job of coaching him to deal with those kind of distractions.

One of the things we did was to have our players verbally abuse him when we held scrimmages to try and simulate what was going to be said when he threw in an official game at one of our rival schools. Our players did it out of love because they wanted to see him get better, but they also knew him better than any fans so they could really get on him in a more irritating way than the fans could.

We would chant the word OVERRATED again and again and make comments about how he was not as good as his father (Doug Drabek 1990 Major League Baseball National League Cy Young Award Winner For Top Pitcher). At first he was surprised at what we came up with. Then as he heard it repeatedly, he became amused and responded beautifully in the best way possible – by pitching better. Come playoff time, Kyle and the team did not let any of that negative stuff faze them. I attribute that positive response to the coaching work we did in scrimmages and in teaching our players how to respond. They did a tremendous job of keeping their composure in big ball games where other teams would have caved in.

## WIN THE NEXT PITCH

Eastman also places heavy emphasis on playing the game one pitch at a time and controlling what you can control, which in baseball is a commitment to playing the next pitch.

We spend a lot of time teaching our players to focus on what they can control, which is spending maximum effort on the next pitch instead of anything else. It's essential that we show them how to do that from day one. We talk about the mental side of the game and in playing with a focus on one pitch at a time early in the season, in scrimmage games, and in everything else we do because that is one of the only things a player has control over.

We have used various tools to help us train the mental game from books like *The Mental Game of Baseball*, *Heads Up Baseball*, and many of Brian Cain's DVDs and CDs to help teach our athletes how to play one pitch at a time. I always knew that the mental part of the game was 75-80%, but rarely taught it that much. Now that I understand how much of a determining factor it is in the development of our athletes, every year it becomes a bigger part of our program.

## TIME IN CLASSROOM AND ON FIELD IMPORTANT

Equally important as going over playing skills on the field is maximizing the use of the classroom environment to introduce and educate athletes about various aspects of the game.

We use the classroom allowing our players to take notes and know exactly what we want them to do. We also will often meet for maybe five to ten minutes before practice and talk about visualization, breathing, our approach at the plate, or a new bunt coverage that we are putting in. We also have study halls so that we can help our athletes be successful in the classroom too.

## STRESS QUALITY OVER QUANTITY
Eastman knows that with the limited time that high schools and colleges have for practice, that the quality of repetitions are more important than the quantity, although ideally both quality and quantity are important.

We stress to our players the value of getting game-like quality repetitions in practice. I would rather see a player take fifteen game-like ground balls and have to make a throw to a base than I would have him take one hundred aerobic ground balls, where he fields them off of a fungo bat and doesn't have to make a throw or use a stopwatch to keep his rhythm and tempo at a game-like pace.

Our facility was named the number one facility in high school baseball in the country and our boosters have done a tremendous job at getting us great cages. I can't tell you the number of times I see players just go in there and hammer away without a plan versus having a clear plan of what they want to do with each swing, and stepping out of the box between pitches just like they are going to do during a live game.

We show them a routine they can use in batting practice or in the bullpen so that when they are playing summer ball or working out with a father or friends, they can take a little bit of a work-smart approach and not just be out there working hard.

## KISS METHOD

Over the years, Eastman has found that the best way to coach is to keep it super simple.

I am a big believer in the K.I.S.S. Principle -- Keep It Super Simple. We do situational hitting everyday but we boil it down to two or three situations we want our players to focus on and we work on those situations only for that day.

On defense we work a lot on making the routine plays. We keep it very basic. We feel that there are just three things that are momentum changers and we work on those three every day at practice. Now we could have 17 different pick off plays and 10 different bunt coverages, but that would be too hard to manage and not simple at all. We keep it very simple so that our players can get very good at a few things and be able to execute them flawlessly and more often.

## CHALLENGING OFF-SEASON WORKOUTS

Eastman and his players feel that one of the things they do that helps them have success is their ability to implement a quality off-season and a year-round workout regimen.

Texas is a big football state. Because of intense competition for players, we don't get as many from the talent pool as we'd like; but the ones who are not playing a fall sport go through our very physically demanding fall program that prepares them well for the season that begins in spring. I also think we do a lot of things that other programs don't or can't do. We have both the facilities to do so and the tremendous support of The Woodlands.

We challenge our players physically and mentally with our workouts and stress to them that championships are won in the off-season, not during spring training. We put a huge emphasis on the quality of the 50 minutes a day of conditioning we engage in, and our players have responded very well.

We practice differently from the way many coaches do with their teams. For example, we do wind sprints instead of distance running. We may make them run long distance mileage to become more mentally tough, but the emphasis of our strength program is on power, speed and explosion over short distances. We also have a long toss throwing program that we do in the off season a few days a week, and we use the weight room for baseball specific exercises. We also try to get a lot done in a short period of time everyday that we are on the field.

The players like the discipline and intensity of the drills and the workouts we do. When it comes to baseball practice, I think that less is more. What I mean is if you can keep it fast paced and moving quickly, you will get more out of your players in a shorter period of time. Don't get me wrong, there are days where we grind and put in the hours, but most of the time we are in and out, as sharp, quick and as efficient as possible.

## SWIMMING POOL WORKOUTS CHALLENGE PLAYERS

Eastman utilizes the swimming pool to challenge his athletes and give them a workout that not a lot of them are accustomed to. He's fortunate to have one of the best swim coaches and programs in Texas.

> We utilize the swimming pool a lot in the fall. It's a break from the baseball practice routine, a great low impact exercise and cardio and strengthening exercise. We use kick boards, plyometrics (bridging the gap between strength and speed), medicine ball exercises, laps and a few other things. The players hate the workout, but they love what it does to their bodies. It gives them a lot of confidence because they get stronger, and it acts to prevent and minimize a lot of shoulder injuries.

## UTILIZE KNOWLEDGE OF OTHER COACHES IN DEPARTMENT

Eastman knows that he is not an expert in all fields, and is always willing to ask for help and advice when it comes to developing workouts and getting instruction.

> I've asked Dan Green, an icon in our track and cross-country programs and very well-known and respected coach, to help with our running form. Dan has been doing this a lot longer than I have and he is about as good as there is in the country as a running coach.

Kent Kirchner, The Woodlands swim coach, helps us with our workouts in the water to make sure that we are doing things that will help us as it relates specifically to baseball.

## PRACTICE ROUTINES – CONSISTENCY BREEDS CONFIDENCE

Having consistency in your practice routine sets the stage for consistency in performance.

We start every day with a dynamic warm-up that takes about 10 minutes and then we go into our throwing program. We want our players working on their rhythm and timing as well as playing quality catch so that they have a target for every throw. We also have players run and chase down a ball if they overthrow their partner while playing catch. This helps them to focus while playing catch.

The time when you are playing catch should be a critical part of your practice. We stress to our players that playing defense is simply quality throw and catch. If you can do those two things, you are going to make most of the routine plays.

We then go into our individual defensive drills. Each position player has things that he does specific to his position. We usually have four coaches because we are practicing our junior varsity and varsity together. Our pitching coach trains just the pitchers, which has been a huge benefit for us to have someone designated as a pitching coach. Even when we had budget cuts, we had someone who specialized in working with our pitchers. I don't think I can stress enough how important it is to have someone with your pitchers every day.

We then go into our team defense and the three things that we focus on are the momentum changers, bunt coverage, cut-offs, and double plays. We are working on one of those momentum changers everyday in some kind of drill work. We try to get through a lot of things in a short amount of time.

Then we go through our hitting routine that includes base running. We try to get the varsity to hit live in practice on the field everyday. We practice a lot of situational hitting in the cages. We also will have a scrimmage game. Whether it is a fungo game, a two- pitch game, or an all out intra-squad, I think the scrimmage has been very big for us in recent years.

## COMPETE EVERYDAY

Setting up drills and practice to include as much competition as possible is a great way to keep players motivated and working at a game-like pace.

We try to compete in everything we do, whether it's against the clock with a stopwatch or a competition between teams. Whatever we're doing, we try to challenge the players and get them competing. Sometimes it is competing with each other in an intra-squad scrimmage, and sometimes it is competing alone against your own best performance in drill work, trying to set a new personal record.

We want our players to compete as much as possible in practice because then there is very little change to what we do when we get into a game. We don't want them changing anything on game day. They shouldn't be trying to "step up" to perform at a level they've never practiced. They need to be doing what they do every day in practice: competing as best they can, playing the game one pitch at a time, and controlling what they can control.

Visit www.ToiletsBricksFishHooksAndPride.com
For FREE Extras, Updates & Information

# CHAPTER 15 | GEORGE HORTON SHARES SUCCESS SECRETS

Think How Good It's Going To Feel

George Horton led the Cal State Fullerton Titans Baseball Team to the 2004 NCAA National Championship and was named the 2003 and 2004 American Baseball Coaches Association National Coach of The Year. I was able to interview him on his approach to the mental game and the difference the mental game made in the Titans championship run.

**BC:** How would you describe your working relationship with sport psychologist Ken Ravizza?

**GH:** Ken and I have worked closely for a long time now. What he brings to our program is a load of experience in teaching the mental game and the ability to relate that part of the game from the classroom to the field.

Ken brings another voice to the team and does a tremendous job in relating to our players what they mentally have to do to be successful. The athletes in the program really enjoy his presence. He was as key an element in the 2004 national championship as anyone else.

**BC:** What mental toughness techniques or exercises had the most impact on the players?

**GH:** The biggest thing was a change in their perspective. In the middle of the season we had gone to Austin, Texas for a series of games and got swept by the (University of Texas) Longhorns. It wasn't even close. Following that, the energy on the team just drained out of them and became as low as I have ever seen it. The staff and players were thinking that this was a rebuilding year and that we were going to struggle, but did not think we would be at 15-16 in the middle of our season. We thought we would be better than that.

Ken came in and talked to the team. The first thing he asked us was what we were doing well. I responded that we were playing good defense, but that was only after I mentally went through a long list of all the things we weren't doing well. I was grasping at straws. It was hard to hide the negatives all of us felt in the room. The next thing he told us was that we had an opportunity to do what no Titans team had ever done before.

Most of our players were thinking, "Yeah, be the first Titans team not to go to the post-season," but what he said was exactly the opposite,". . . be the first Titan team to go from under .500 at the middle of the season, to being national champions." That really caught everyone's attention.

He then asked our players to "Think how good it is going to feel when you get to Omaha?" From that point, you could really see a weight lifted off everyone's backs. P.J. Pillittere, one of our veteran players, would write that saying, "Think how good it is going to feel," on the dugout wall. Everybody rallied around that saying.

At mid-season, we were all caught up in the results and since we were not getting the results we wanted, we started to press. In baseball, as in every team sport, you have no control over the results since there are two teams trying to outsmart each other and many moving parts; so all you
c                                    a                                    n

do is play one pitch at a time and work the process. After that wake up call, we all got back to the process with quality at-bats, quality pitches and playing the game one pitch at a time. I think that helped turn the season around for us.

**BC:** Talk about that championship season and what factors you attribute to turning around that season.

**GH:** I think a lot of the stuff that we talked about before made the difference for us -- changing the collective perspective, getting back to the process, focusing more on one pitch at a time and controlling what we could control.

I think another important factor was that our athletes continued to work very hard every day. Dave Serrano, Rick Vanderhook and Chad Baum of our coaching staff did a great job of staying on top of the fundamental work that needed to happen every day with our players.

We had a very special group of Titans that year, and I think that their chemistry on and off the field also helped us to turn the season around. They were a very close-knit group of players in that they all pulled for each other. It didn't matter who was at the plate or on the mound. We had all 25 players pulling in the same direction, and when you get that going, special things will happen.

**BC:** How did you as a coaching staff reinforce those techniques that Ken was teaching?

**GH:** Our staff had been working well together for a long time, so there were no surprises there. But you know how crazy and hectic the day-to-day operations of a baseball program can get when you are in the middle of your season. In the 2004 season, we were very distracted by our lack of results and somehow inadvertently put aside talking up and reinforcing the mental game.

We were at such a low point that I knew of nothing else to try than to bring Ken in to work with our program again. When he came in, he said things that he had probably said before, but they really sank in this time. We really made a conscious effort to reinforce the techniques that Ken was talking about. We would spend more time talking about each of our players' routines and the importance of taking that good deep breath as the pitcher becomes set and ready to throw, or as the hitter gets into the batter's box and prepares to swing. I think as a staff we also did a better job of flushing the negatives and getting on with thinking about the next pitch. As a coach you need to model what you want from your players to the extent that they must witness your behavior with their own eyes, the behavior you would like to see them adopt and by this behavior I mean actually demonstrating the most helpful step-by-step processes.

**BC:** What factors do you attribute to the consistent level of success at your program?

**GH:** I think there were a lot of factors that contributed to the levels of success that Cal State Fullerton Baseball achieved. It all started well before I got here with the previous Titans setting a high standard of excellence. There was a lot of pride and tradition in being able to wear Titans across your chest. Every time our athletes suited up to go and play, we reminded them that they represented not only themselves and the team but all the former Titans that have gone through our program.

I think our players worked as hard day-in-and-day-out as anyone in the country. We took a lot of pride in getting better every day. We also worked very hard on the fundamentals. We emphasized the little things every day -- bunting, base running, and execution -- all the little things that we relied heavily upon in games to be successful.

We also tried to transform our practices as close to game conditions as possible. When we scrimmaged, we often started with runners on base and used the scoreboard to establish a more realistic game psychology. We also were able to recruit great talent that helped to make our intra-squad practices all that much more competitive because we believed each player must compete everyday to win a position.

**BC:** Once you climbed to the peak and were at the top of college baseball, how did you challenge the team and program to maintain that level of excellence?

**GH:** We challenged our athletes the same way whether we were coming off a national championship season or a season in which we fell short of our goals. The challenge was to get better every day by having quality at-bats, throwing quality pitches and making the fundamental defensive plays. The consistent execution of the things you can control in baseball and that is what we wanted our players to strive for.

In baseball there is a lot of failure in the sense that players don't get hits every time they take a bat, nor do pitchers get every player out, nor do fielders play error-free defense all the time. If you focus on the results and lose sight of the steps in the process, you will find yourself carrying the weight of the world, lots of mental bricks, and not playing up to your potential.

The challenge is to play the game the right way each pitch. That is a lot harder said than done, and is something that we worked on to reach perfection every single day. The team that wins the most pitches is usually the team that wins the game. We focus on the details and doing the little things very well. That is the standard that previous Titans teams have set and the level that we strive for every season.

**BC:** Do you ever change the way you are preparing a team during the season if things aren't going as well as hoped for?

**GH:** We've spent a lot of time preparing for the unexpected. We've often asked umpires to make bad calls on purpose in scrimmages so that we can see how our players respond, and most importantly, so that we can teach our players how we wanted them to respond.

If things were not going as planned, we made changes. The key to peak performance and sustaining success is being able to compensate and adjust; it's not about being perfect. Perfection is a double-edged sword. While it motivates an athlete to do better, it is also a constant source of criticism zapping you of the confidence it takes to have a better performance.

A lot of the athletes that have been on our team have never really failed in athletics before. Many of them were the best players in their high school and in their state, so when they arrived here they got a rude awakening when they realized that the game was played faster by players as good or better than they were. It's as if they were playing a brand new game at a higher, more refined and complex level, which of course was true. Underscoring this point, the older, more seasoned players on the team viewed the incoming freshmen as inexperienced and unpolished and tried to help them get better while they needed to focus on getting themselves better.

**BC:** Is the will to win inherent in all players or are there things a coach can do to bring that desire out of an individual?

**GH:** That's a great question -- a question that I often think about and discuss with my colleagues. No, I don't believe the will to win is inherent in all players. On the other hand, I don't think very many players who lack the will to win are playing high level college baseball because: you have to really want to win to survive here. Cruising on natural talent is not enough. On the other hand, you can't win on the will-to-win alone. You need more. Here the will to prepare is VITAL to winning besides having physical talent and skills.

I think one big reason that our athletes prepare and practice so hard is because they feel they deserve to win every time they step on the field. In part, we have the previous Titans to thank for this. Those great historic teams were able to establish a level of competitiveness and excellence that still inspires and brings out the best in our current teams.

Although we are constantly looking for new ways to motivate our players, we have found that one of the best basic ways is trial-by-fire under the influence and pressure of pure competition. Whether it is in the weight room or an intra-squad scrimmage, our players have demonstrated time and again that they want to compete. Competition for them is a testing of their own mettle. By this I mean they want to see how good they are as individuals and competition is a good way of finding out.

**BC:** What common traits did your NCAA championship teams possess that helped them become champions?

**GH:** The common traits that our NCAA championship teams had was discipline, a desire to get better every day and a focus on the fundamentals of the game. In addition, our championship teams pushed each other hard to get better through head-to-head competition. On top of all that, I think there was a confidence and a belief that they could be champions. It was almost like being born a thoroughbred. They already knew they had championship pedigree within them so all they had to do was to finalize the last step.

Our championship teams also played the game one pitch at a time and focused on the things that they could control.

There was not a lot of talk about the being drafted in the major leagues and things that were out of their control. They focused on simply getting better every day and controlling what we could control. We have had a lot of Titan teams that have taken this same approach and not won the national championship. Sometimes the game rewards you and sometimes it doesn't.

**BC:** Is there any benefit to a pep talk before a game? If yes, when is it appropriate?

**GH:** I'm not a big believer in pep talks before games because I think it can get players overly emotional, too excited and raise their expectations too unreasonably high. If anything, I think I try to get our players to relax before a game. At our level, success is all about consistency and doing what you do on a daily basis in practice in games. That is why our practice time is so important.

We want our players to play at their pace and to treat every game like a practice, and every practice like a game so that nothing changes. Our goal is to play Titan Baseball and let everything else take care of itself. We are going to throw strikes, play catch and put the ball in play. If we can do that with a singular focus on the process, in the present moment with a positive mindset, we are giving ourselves the best chance to be successful.

**BC:** What is your recruiting philosophy?

**GH:** Our recruiting philosophy is that we are looking for a player with the best mixture of talent, character and skill to play the game the right way. There are a lot of players out there that have great talent but can become a cancer to the team because they are all about themselves. We have been successful because we have had Titans who take pride in being a great team player, not because we have had superstar individuals.

We are as up front and honest as we can be with the young men we recruit. There are a lot of stories about prospects who are told one thing in the recruiting process, only to be told something different by the staff and players when they got to college. We try to put it all out there up-front so that the player and his family know exactly what to expect if they decide to become a Titan.

We emphasize the importance of getting an education and taking advantage of what the university has to offer as well as the expectations and time commitment that come with being a Titan Baseball player.

We also have our current Titans spend as much time with each prospective recruit as possible so that they can get a feel for each other. Our players have often given our staff great insight about a recruit that helps us to make a decision. Our staff takes what our current Titans say very seriously because our players will be spending the next year or more with the new recruits. They know the tradition and performance expectations that come with wearing the Titan jersey, the privilege and honor that comes with that distinction and take all of that very seriously.

**BC:** What advice would you give to the young coaches reading this book?

**GH:** I think the best place to start is to find a person who can be a mentor for you -- a person who is in a position or a place that you would like to go. I have been blessed to have worked with and alongside some of the best minds in baseball -- Augie Garrido, Dave Snow, Wally Kincaid, Rick Vanderhook, Dave Serrano and Ken Ravizza. Brian Cain is one of those people that can be your mentor.

I also would recommend attending coaching clinics to become a more dedicated student of the game. I learn something new about the game or about a way to run my program through these clinics. That's what makes baseball and coaching so much fun is that you will never know everything about the game and the profession. That's what keeps me motivated -- the chance that I will learn something new and the pursuit of getting better each and every day.

Visit www.ToiletsBricksFishHooksAndPride.com
For FREE Extras, Updates & Information

# PART III

## Motivational Material

# CHAPTER 16 | ATTITUDE = ALTITUDE

### Attitude is a Decision
### By Charles Swindall

The longer I live, the more I realize the impact of attitude on life. Attitude to me is more important than facts. It is more important than the past, than education, than money, than circumstances, than failures, than successes, than what other people think, say, or do. It is more important than appearance, giftedness, or skill. It will make or break a company... a team... a home. The remarkable thing is we have a choice every day regarding the attitude we will embrace for that day. We cannot change our past... we cannot change the fact that people will act in a certain way. We cannot change the inevitable. The one thing we can do is play on the one string we have, and that is our attitude... I am convinced that life is 10% what happens to me and 90% how I react to it. And so it is with you... we are in charge of attitudes.

*"The attitude you take is a decision you make. What kind of attitude will you choose to take today?* **Attitude is a Decision**. *Attitude = Altitude"*

Visit www.ToiletsBricksFishHooksAndPride.com
For FREE Extras, Updates & Information

# CHAPTER 17 | THE ONLY MATH YOU NEED TO KNOW

## What Makes Up 100% in Life

What makes 100%? What does it mean to give MORE than 100%? Ever wonder about those people who say they are giving more than 100%? We have all been to those meetings where someone wants you to give over 100%. How about achieving 110%? What makes up 100% in life?

Here's a little mathematical formula that might help you answer these questions:

*If:*
A B C D E F G H I J K L M N O P Q R S T U V W X Y Z
is *represented as:*
1 2 3 4 5 6 7 8 9 10 11 12 13 14 15 16 17 18 19 20 21 22 23 24 25 26.

*Then:*
K-N-O-W-L-E-D-G-E =
11+14+15+23+12+5+4+7+5 = 96%

H-A-R-D-W-O-R-K =
8+1+18+4+23+15+18+11 = 98%

A-T-T-I-T-U-D-E =
1+20+20+9+20+21+4+5 = 100%

*So, one can conclude with mathematical certainty that while knowledge and hard work will get you close to where you want to go, attitude will absolutely get you there. You can control your attitude and that is what it takes to be great. Attitude is a decision and your attitude will determine your altitude.*

*If you are looking for a computer program that will turn letters into numbers so that you can use this same concept to motivate your team, Cain has created this program for you. Visit www. briancain.com and contact Cain on the contact us page for more information.*

# CHAPTER 18 | TEAM WORKING

Ahuman resource executive went out in the field to determine how laborers felt about their work. He went to a building site at your school on today's date.

He approached the first worker and asked, "What are you doing?"

The worker snapped back, "Are you blind? I'm cutting these boulders with primitive tools and putting them together the way the boss told me. I'm sweating under this blazing sun, its backbreaking work, and it's boring me to death!"

The human resource executive quickly backed off and retreated to a second worker. He asked the same question: "What are you doing?"

The worker replied, "I'm shaping these boulders into useable forms, which are then assembled according to the architect's plans. It's family. It's a job. It could be worse."

Somewhat encouraged, the human resources executive went to a third worker. "And what are you doing?," he asked.

"Why can't you see?," beamed the worker as he lifted his arms to the sky, "I'm on a cathedral building team."

***Attitude is a decision****. What attitude will you bring to the team today? Are you part of a team, willing to do what is best for the group, or are you just doing it because someone wants you to? If you get nothing else out of reading this book, get this…*

*You are responsible for your attitude, thoughts and actions. Nothing can take away the responsibility and the control I have over myself which I possess as a human being.*

**Nicole Ludwig**

# CHAPTER 19 | COFFEE GOOD FOR YOUR HEALTH

Boiling May Become You

A young woman went to her mother and told her about her life and how things were hard for her. She did not know how she was going to make it and wanted to give up. She was tired of fighting and struggling. It seemed as soon as one problem was solved a new one arose.

Her mother took her into the kitchen. She filled three pots with water. In the first pot, she placed carrots, in the second pot she placed eggs and in the last pot she placed ground coffee beans. Then she let them sit and boil without saying a word. In about twenty minutes she turned off the burners. She fished the carrots out and placed them in one bowl. She pulled the eggs out and placed them in another bowl. Then she ladled the coffee into a third bowl. Turning to her daughter, she asked, "Tell me what you see?" "Carrots, eggs, and coffee," her daughter replied. She brought her daughter closer and asked her to feel the carrots. Her daughter did and noted that they felt soft. Her mother then asked her to take an egg and break it. She did exactly that and after pulling off the shell, she observed a hard-boiled egg. Finally, she asked her daughter to sip the coffee. The daughter smiled, as she tasted its rich aroma.

The daughter then asked, "What's the point, mom?" Her mother explained that each of these objects had faced the same adversity (boiling water), but each reacted differently. The carrot went in strong, hard and unrelenting. After being subjected to the boiling water, it softened and became weak. The egg had been fragile. Its thin outer shell had protected its liquid interior. After sitting through the boiling water, its inside became hardened. The ground coffee beans were unique, however. After they were in the boiling water they had changed the water.

"Which are you"? she asked her daughter. "When adversity knocks on your door, how do you respond? Are you a carrot, an egg, or a coffee bean?"

Now think of this: Which are you?

Are you the carrot that seems strong, but with pain and adversity, do you wilt and become soft and lose your strength?

Are you the egg that starts with a malleable heart, but changes with the heat? Do you have a fluid spirit, but after a loss, not playing well, getting put on the bench, or some other trial, do you become hardened and stiff? Does your shell look the same, but on the inside are you bitter and tough with a stiff spirit and a hardened heart?

Or are you like the coffee bean? The bean actually changed the hot water, the very element that brings the pain. When the water gets hot, it releases the fragrance and flavor. If you are like the bean, when things are at their worst, you get better and change the situation around you. When the hours are the darkest and trials are their greatest, do you elevate to another level?

How do you handle Adversity? ARE YOU A CARROT, AN EGG, OR A COFFEE BEAN?

*"How will you respond to the pressure situation and the adversity that you will face this season? Will you get encouraged or*

# CHAPTER 20 | STANDING IN THE EYE OF THE STORM

### After Getting Up Off The Mat

I t's a RARE PERSON who doesn't get discouraged in the face of adversity. Whether it happens to us or to a friend we're trying to cheer up, the answer to overcoming adversity lies in one word: PERSEVERANCE. The value of courage, persistence, and perseverance has rarely been illustrated more convincingly than in the life story of this man, his age appears in the column on the right.

| ADVERSITY | AGE |
|---|---|
| Failed in business | 22 |
| Ran for Legislature—defeated | 23 |
| Failed again in business | 24 |
| Elected to Legislature | 25 |
| Sweetheart died | 26 |
| Had a nervous breakdown | 27 |
| Defeated for Speaker | 29 |
| Defeated for Elector | 31 |
| Defeated for Congress | 34 |
| Elected to Congress | 37 |
| Defeated for Congress | 39 |
| Defeated for Senate | 46 |
| Defeated for Vice President | 47 |
| Defeated for Senate | 49 |
| Elected President of the United States | 51 |

That's the record of Abraham Lincoln!

*You may be disappointed if you fail, but you are doomed if you don't try. Failure is not in losing the game, but in not getting off the mat when you are knocked down. How do you respond to adversity? What are specific examples of times when you have fought back in the face of adversity?*

Visit www.ToiletsBricksFishHooksAndPride.com
For FREE Extras, Updates & Information

# CHAPTER 21 | IT COULDN'T BE DONE

So He Started to Sing As He Tackled The Thing
— Edgar A. Guest

Somebody said that it couldn't be done
But with a chuckle he replied
That "maybe it couldn't," but he would be one
Who wouldn't say so 'til he'd tried.
So he buckled right in with the trace of a grin on his face.
If he worried, he hid it.
He started to sing as he tackled the thing
That couldn't be done, and he did it.
Somebody scoffed: "oh, you'll never do that;
At least no one has ever done it,"
But he took off his coat and he took off his hat,
And the first thing we knew, he'd begun it.
With a lift of his chin and a bit of a grin
Without any doubting or quitting,
He started to sing as he tackled the thing
That couldn't be done, and he did it.
There are thousands to tell you it cannot be done.
There are thousands to prophesy failure.
There are thousands to point out to you, one by one,
The dangers that wait to assail you.
But just buckle right in with a bit of a grin.
Just take off your coat and go to it;
Just start to sing as you tackle the thing
That cannot be done, and you'll do it.

# CHAPTER 22 | THE GUY IN THE GLASS

He's The Fellow to Please
Peter "Dale" Winbrow Sr (1895-1954)

When you get what you want in your struggle for pelf
And the world makes you King for a day,
Then go to your mirror and look at yourself
And see what that guy has to say.

For it isn't your Father or Mother or Wife
Whose judgment upon you must pass,
But the feller whose verdict counts most in this life
Is the guy staring back from the glass.

He's the feller to please, never mind all the rest,
For he's with you clear up to the end,
And you've passed your most dangerous and difficult test
If the guy in the glass is your friend.

You may be like Jack Horner and "chisel" a plum,
And think that you're a wonderful guy,
But the guy in the glass says you're only a bum
If you can't look him straight in the eye.

You may fool the whole world down the pathway of years
And get pats on the back as you pass,
But your final reward will be heartache and tears
If you've cheated the guy in the glass.

*I first heard this poem at a football banquet when I was a sophomore in high school. It has stayed with me ever since. It has helped me to realize that YOU are in control of your own destiny and that YOUR success in life is most greatly influenced by YOU and YOUR actions. What do you see when you look in the glass?*

Visit www.ToiletsBricksFishHooksAndPride.com
For FREE Extras, Updates & Information

# CHAPTER 23 | THE FOUNTAIN VS. THE DRAIN

## Let Me Do It For You Or It's Not My Job

The Fountain is always part of the answer.

The Drain is always part of the problem.

The Fountain always has a system.

The Drain always has an excuse.

The Fountain says, "Let me do it for you."

The Drain says, "That's not my job."

The Fountain sees an answer for every problem.

The Drain sees a problem for every answer.

The Fountain sees a green near every sand trap.

The Drain sees two or three sand traps near every green.

The Fountain says "It may be difficult, but it's possible."

The Drain said, "It may be possible, but it's too difficult."

*It is real simple. If you want to be a good teammate and if you want people to like you, you MUST be a fountain. Your team does not need drains. Drains only clog things up.*

# CHAPTER 24 | TOMORROW

Too Bad Indeed He Was Busy Today
Edgar Guest

He said he was going to be all that a mortal could be, tomorrow.

None would be braver and stronger than he, tomorrow.

A friend who was weary had trouble he knew, needed a lift and wanted one too, gave him a call to see what he could do, tomorrow.

He stacked up the letters he would read, tomorrow.

He thought of the friends he would write, tomorrow.

It was too bad indeed he was busy today, but had a moment to stop on the way, more time I'll give to others he would say, tomorrow.

The greatest of workers this man would have been, tomorrow.

And the world would have known him had he ever seen tomorrow.

But the fact is that he died and faded from view, and all that he left when his living was through, was a mountain of things to do.

Tomorrow.

*Do not wait until tomorrow to start preparing for this season.*

*Tomorrow never comes. It is the start that stops most people. Start today.*

*Your career and more importantly your life is the sum of your todays.*

*TODAY + TODAY + TODAY = Your Career & Your Life*

**Nicole Ludwig**

# CHAPTER 25 | WE ALL SHARE ONE BANK

Yesterday Is A Cancelled Check.
Today Is Cash.

Athletic Bank Account For     _____

*(Your Name Here)*

If you had a bank that credited your account each morning with $86,400.00 that carried over no balance from day to day – allowed you to keep no cash in your account – and every evening cancelled whatever part of the amount you had failed to use during the day – WHAT WOULD YOU DO? Draw out every cent, of course, and use it to your advantage, RIGHT?

Well, YOU HAVE such a bank – and its name is TIME TO PARTICIPATE IN ATHLETICS. Every morning, it credits you with 86,400 seconds. Every night, it writes off as lost whatever of this balance you have failed to invest in preparing for your next game or season.

The bank carries over no balances and it allows no overdrafts. It opens a new account with you each day and it burns the record of the day each night. If you fail to use the day's deposits, the loss of preparation for your next opportunity to play is yours. There's no going back.

There is no drawing against the "Tomorrow." It is up to you to invest this precious fund of hours, minutes and seconds in order to get the utmost out of your physical talent, mental capabilities, knowledge of the game, and the confidence that comes with not counting the days, but making the days count.

**ONLY YOU AND TIME WILL DETERMINE YOUR DESTINATION AND THE DIFFERENCE YOU WILL MAKE IN YOUR NEXT COMPETITION.**

Ask your players and staff, "What will you do today to get better?" Remember that yesterday is history, tomorrow is a mystery and that today is your gift. That is why we call it the present. It has also been said that yesterday is a canceled check, tomorrow is a promissory note, and today is cash. Spend it wisely!

Visit www.ToiletsBricksFishHooksAndPride.com
For FREE Extras, Updates & Information

# WHO IS BRIAN CAIN?
## About The Author

Brian M. Cain, MS, CMAA, is an expert in the area of Mental Conditioning, Peak Performance Coaching, and Applied Sport Psychology. He has worked with coaches, athletes, and teams at the Olympic level and in the National Football League (NFL), National Basketball Association (NBA), National Hockey League (NHL), Ultimate Fighting Championship (UFC), and Major League Baseball (MLB) on using mental conditioning to perform at their best when it means the most.

Cain has also worked with programs in some of the top college athletic departments around the country, including the University of Alabama, Auburn University, Florida State University, the University of Iowa, the University of Maryland, the University of Mississippi, Mississippi State University, Oregon State University, the University of

Southern California, the University of Tennessee, Texas Christian University, Vanderbilt University, Washington State University, Yale University, and many others.

Cain has worked as a mental-conditioning consultant with numerous high school-, state-, and national-championship programs. He has delivered his award-winning seminars and presentations at coaches' clinics, leadership summits, and athletic directors' conventions all over the country. As a high-school athletic director, he is one of the youngest ever to receive the Certified Master Athletic Administration Certification from the National Interscholastic Athletic Administrators Association.

A highly sought-after Peak Performance Coach, clinician, and keynote and motivational speaker, Cain delivers his message with passion, enthusiasm, and in an engaging style that keeps his audiences entertained while being educated. Someone who lives what he teaches, Cain will inspire you and give you the tools necessary to get the most out of your career.

Find out when Cain will be coming to your area by visiting his calendar at **www.briancain.com**.

# HOW YOU CAN BECOME
# A MASTER OF THE MENTAL GAME
CAIN OFFERS A RANGE OF TRAINING MATERIALS TO GET YOU
OR YOUR TEAM TO THE TOP OF YOUR GAME.
AVAILABLE AT WWW.BRIANCAIN.COM

## MASTERS OF THE MENTAL GAME SERIES BOOKS

### Champions Tell All:
### Inexpensive Experience From The Worlds Best
Cain provides you with all access to some of the World's greatest
performers. Learn from mixed martial arts world champions and
college All-Americans about mental toughness.

### The Daily Dominator:
### Perform Your Best Today. Every Day!
You get 366 Daily Mental Conditioning lessons to help you start
your day down the path to excellence. Investing time each day
with Cain is your best way to become your best self.

### The Mental Conditioning Manual:
### Your Blueprint For Excellence
This is the exact system Cain uses to build champions and masters
of the mental game and has helped produce NCAA and High
School, champions, MMA world champions, and more.

### So What, Next Pitch:
### How To Play Your Best When It Means The Most
A compilation of interviews with top coaches and players where
Cain teaches you their systems and tricks. Learn from the insights
of these masters of the mental game.

### Toilets Bricks Fish Hooks and PRIDE:
### The Peak Performance Toolbox EXPOSED
Go inside the most successful programs in the country that use
Cain's Peak Performance System. Use this book to unlock your
potential and learn to play your best when it means the most.

# PEAK PERFORMANCE TRAINING TOOLS

## The Peak Performance System: (P.R.I.D.E.) Personal Responsibility In Daily Excellence

This big, video-based training program is Cain's signature training program for coaches, athletes and teams. It will take you step by step to the top of the performance mountain.

## Diamond Domination Training : The New 4RIP3 System for Baseball and Softball

This training program is being used by 11 teams in the NCAA top 25 in college baseball and 8 of the top 25 in college softball. It will help you and your team to unlock your potential and play the best baseball and softball of your life.

## 4RIP3 MMA Mental Conditioning System

Get the techniques used by the best fighters in the world to and start bringing the fighter you are in the gym into the cage. It will help you unlock your potential, teach you drills to sharpen your focus and give you the confidence of a champion

## The Peak Performance Boot Camp

This introductory program will give you the tools, power, and mental toughness you need to be prepared for every game, every play, and every minute. Learn techniques to get the absolute best chance of maximizing your potential and getting the most out of your ability.

### And more at www.BrianCain.com/products

*"Cain has tapped into the mental side of performance like no one ever has."*

**Tom Murphy**
**President, The Fitness Zone Gym**

*"This is your blueprint for making excellence a lifestyle not an event."*

**Jim Schlossnagle**
**2010 National College Baseball Coach of The Year**

*"Cain's books, DVDs and audio programs will give you a formula for success between the ears."*

**Bob Tewksbury**
**Sport Psychology Consultant, Boston Red Sox**

*"If you make one investment in coaching excellence and impacting the lives of the youth you lead, this is the program you want to follow."*

**Clay Chournous**
**High School Football and Baseball Coach, Bear River H.S.**

*"This will not only help you on the field, it will help you in life."*

**Nate Yeskie**
**Assistant Baseball Coach, Oregon State University**

*"Brian Cain will give you and your team a system for playing at your best when it means the most."*

**Todd Whitting**
**Head Baseball Coach, Univ. of Houston**

*"This was the best presentation I have seen in all of my clinics/ conventions I have attended over the years. OUTSTANDING!!!"*

**Michelle Daddona**
**Riverside Community College**

*"The information you get from Brian is the highest quality and can benefit a team, an athletic department and coaches of all experience levels."*

**Bill Gray**
**Missouri Southern State University**

## CONNECT WITH CAIN

Your link to doing a little a lot, not a lot a little

*twitter.com/briancainpeak*

*facebook.com/briancainpeak*

*linkedin.com/in/briancainpeak*

*youtube.com/wwwbriancaincom*

*briancain.com/podcast*

## SIGN UP FOR THE
## PEAK PERFORMANCE NEWSLETTER

Cain's newsletter is full of information to help you unlock your potential and perform at your best when it means the most. Subscribe for free and get a bonus audio training.
**www.BrianCain.com/newsletter**

## VISIT CAIN ON THE WEB

## www.BrianCain.com

**Remember to go to
www.BrianCain.com/experience
for all the BONUS Mental Conditioning
material mentioned in this book.**

## Brian Cain Peak Performance, LLC

www.BrianCain.com
www.BrianCainInnerCircle.com
www.ToiletsBricksFishHooksAndPride.com
www.SoWhatNextPitch.com
www.MentalConditioningManual.com

| 39 | 48 | 59 | 28 | 71 | 26 | 34 | 70 | 95 | 06 |
| 21 | 91 | 42 | 12 | 30 | 84 | 76 | 97 | 61 | 75 |
| 58 | 08 | 85 | 32 | 45 | 66 | 36 | 63 | 23 | 29 |
| 96 | 80 | 00 | 88 | 89 | 11 | 25 | 57 | 02 | 90 |
| 74 | 33 | 56 | 93 | 52 | 73 | 04 | 10 | 49 | 19 |
| 87 | 09 | 16 | 81 | 69 | 38 | 64 | 50 | 83 | 41 |
| 31 | 01 | 40 | 47 | 18 | 77 | 24 | 14 | 13 | 60 |
| 79 | 72 | 05 | 51 | 82 | 55 | 15 | 17 | 44 | 94 |
| 54 | 35 | 53 | 68 | 65 | 20 | 03 | 99 | 86 | 27 |
| 67 | 46 | 07 | 78 | 22 | 92 | 37 | 62 | 98 | 43 |

## Brian Cain Peak Performance, LLC

www.BrianCain.com
www.BrianCainInnerCircle.com
www.ToiletsBricksFishHooksAndPride.com
www.SoWhatNextPitch.com
www.MentalConditioningManual.com

| 39 | 48 | 59 | 28 | 71 | 26 | 34 | 70 | 95 | 06 |
| 21 | 91 | 42 | 12 | 30 | 84 | 76 | 97 | 61 | 75 |
| 58 | 08 | 85 | 32 | 45 | 66 | 36 | 63 | 23 | 29 |
| 96 | 80 | 00 | 88 | 89 | 11 | 25 | 57 | 02 | 90 |
| 74 | 33 | 56 | 93 | 52 | 73 | 04 | 10 | 49 | 19 |
| 87 | 09 | 16 | 81 | 69 | 38 | 64 | 50 | 83 | 41 |
| 31 | 01 | 40 | 47 | 18 | 77 | 24 | 14 | 13 | 60 |
| 79 | 72 | 05 | 51 | 82 | 55 | 15 | 17 | 44 | 94 |
| 54 | 35 | 53 | 68 | 65 | 20 | 03 | 99 | 86 | 27 |
| 67 | 46 | 07 | 78 | 22 | 92 | 37 | 62 | 98 | 43 |

## Brian Cain Peak Performance, LLC

www.BrianCain.com
www.BrianCainInnerCircle.com
www.ToiletsBricksFishHooksAndPride.com
www.SoWhatNextPitch.com
www.MentalConditioningManual.com

| 39 | 48 | 59 | 28 | 71 | 26 | 34 | 70 | 95 | 06 |
|----|----|----|----|----|----|----|----|----|----|
| 21 | 91 | 42 | 12 | 30 | 84 | 76 | 97 | 61 | 75 |
| 58 | 08 | 85 | 32 | 45 | 66 | 36 | 63 | 23 | 29 |
| 96 | 80 | 00 | 88 | 89 | 11 | 25 | 57 | 02 | 90 |
| 74 | 33 | 56 | 93 | 52 | 73 | 04 | 10 | 49 | 19 |
| 87 | 09 | 16 | 81 | 69 | 38 | 64 | 50 | 83 | 41 |
| 31 | 01 | 40 | 47 | 18 | 77 | 24 | 14 | 13 | 60 |
| 79 | 72 | 05 | 51 | 82 | 55 | 15 | 17 | 44 | 94 |
| 54 | 35 | 53 | 68 | 65 | 20 | 03 | 99 | 86 | 27 |
| 67 | 46 | 07 | 78 | 22 | 92 | 37 | 62 | 98 | 43 |

## Brian Cain Peak Performance, LLC

www.BrianCain.com
www.BrianCainInnerCircle.com
www.ToiletsBricksFishHooksAndPride.com
www.SoWhatNextPitch.com
www.MentalConditioningManual.com

| 39 | 48 | 59 | 28 | 71 | 26 | 34 | 70 | 95 | 06 |
|----|----|----|----|----|----|----|----|----|----|
| 21 | 91 | 42 | 12 | 30 | 84 | 76 | 97 | 61 | 75 |
| 58 | 08 | 85 | 32 | 45 | 66 | 36 | 63 | 23 | 29 |
| 96 | 80 | 00 | 88 | 89 | 11 | 25 | 57 | 02 | 90 |
| 74 | 33 | 56 | 93 | 52 | 73 | 04 | 10 | 49 | 19 |
| 87 | 09 | 16 | 81 | 69 | 38 | 64 | 50 | 83 | 41 |
| 31 | 01 | 40 | 47 | 18 | 77 | 24 | 14 | 13 | 60 |
| 79 | 72 | 05 | 51 | 82 | 55 | 15 | 17 | 44 | 94 |
| 54 | 35 | 53 | 68 | 65 | 20 | 03 | 99 | 86 | 27 |

## Brian Cain Peak Performance, LLC

www.BrianCain.com
www.BrianCainInnerCircle.com
www.ToiletsBricksFishHooksAndPride.com
www.SoWhatNextPitch.com
www.MentalConditioningManual.com

| 39 | 48 | 59 | 28 | 71 | 26 | 34 | 70 | 95 | 06 |
| 21 | 91 | 42 | 12 | 30 | 84 | 76 | 97 | 61 | 75 |
| 58 | 08 | 85 | 32 | 45 | 66 | 36 | 63 | 23 | 29 |
| 96 | 80 | 00 | 88 | 89 | 11 | 25 | 57 | 02 | 90 |
| 74 | 33 | 56 | 93 | 52 | 73 | 04 | 10 | 49 | 19 |
| 87 | 09 | 16 | 81 | 69 | 38 | 64 | 50 | 83 | 41 |
| 31 | 01 | 40 | 47 | 18 | 77 | 24 | 14 | 13 | 60 |
| 79 | 72 | 05 | 51 | 82 | 55 | 15 | 17 | 44 | 94 |
| 54 | 35 | 53 | 68 | 65 | 20 | 03 | 99 | 86 | 27 |
| 67 | 46 | 07 | 78 | 22 | 92 | 37 | 62 | 98 | 43 |

## Brian Cain Peak Performance, LLC

www.BrianCain.com
www.BrianCainInnerCircle.com
www.ToiletsBricksFishHooksAndPride.com
www.SoWhatNextPitch.com
www.MentalConditioningManual.com

| 39 | 48 | 59 | 28 | 71 | 26 | 34 | 70 | 95 | 06 |
| 21 | 91 | 42 | 12 | 30 | 84 | 76 | 97 | 61 | 75 |
| 58 | 08 | 85 | 32 | 45 | 66 | 36 | 63 | 23 | 29 |
| 96 | 80 | 00 | 88 | 89 | 11 | 25 | 57 | 02 | 90 |
| 74 | 33 | 56 | 93 | 52 | 73 | 04 | 10 | 49 | 19 |
| 87 | 09 | 16 | 81 | 69 | 38 | 64 | 50 | 83 | 41 |
| 31 | 01 | 40 | 47 | 18 | 77 | 24 | 14 | 13 | 60 |
| 79 | 72 | 05 | 51 | 82 | 55 | 15 | 17 | 44 | 94 |
| 54 | 35 | 53 | 68 | 65 | 20 | 03 | 99 | 86 | 27 |

## Brian Cain Peak Performance, LLC

www.BrianCain.com
www.BrianCainInnerCircle.com
www.ToiletsBricksFishHooksAndPride.com
www.SoWhatNextPitch.com
www.MentalConditioningManual.com

| 39 | 48 | 59 | 28 | 71 | 26 | 34 | 70 | 95 | 06 |
|----|----|----|----|----|----|----|----|----|----|
| 21 | 91 | 42 | 12 | 30 | 84 | 76 | 97 | 61 | 75 |
| 58 | 08 | 85 | 32 | 45 | 66 | 36 | 63 | 23 | 29 |
| 96 | 80 | 00 | 88 | 89 | 11 | 25 | 57 | 02 | 90 |
| 74 | 33 | 56 | 93 | 52 | 73 | 04 | 10 | 49 | 19 |
| 87 | 09 | 16 | 81 | 69 | 38 | 64 | 50 | 83 | 41 |
| 31 | 01 | 40 | 47 | 18 | 77 | 24 | 14 | 13 | 60 |
| 79 | 72 | 05 | 51 | 82 | 55 | 15 | 17 | 44 | 94 |
| 54 | 35 | 53 | 68 | 65 | 20 | 03 | 99 | 86 | 27 |
| 67 | 46 | 07 | 78 | 22 | 92 | 37 | 62 | 98 | 43 |

## Brian Cain Peak Performance, LLC

www.BrianCain.com
www.BrianCainInnerCircle.com
www.ToiletsBricksFishHooksAndPride.com
www.SoWhatNextPitch.com
www.MentalConditioningManual.com

| 39 | 48 | 59 | 28 | 71 | 26 | 34 | 70 | 95 | 06 |
|----|----|----|----|----|----|----|----|----|----|
| 21 | 91 | 42 | 12 | 30 | 84 | 76 | 97 | 61 | 75 |
| 58 | 08 | 85 | 32 | 45 | 66 | 36 | 63 | 23 | 29 |
| 96 | 80 | 00 | 88 | 89 | 11 | 25 | 57 | 02 | 90 |
| 74 | 33 | 56 | 93 | 52 | 73 | 04 | 10 | 49 | 19 |
| 87 | 09 | 16 | 81 | 69 | 38 | 64 | 50 | 83 | 41 |
| 31 | 01 | 40 | 47 | 18 | 77 | 24 | 14 | 13 | 60 |
| 79 | 72 | 05 | 51 | 82 | 55 | 15 | 17 | 44 | 94 |
| 54 | 35 | 53 | 68 | 65 | 20 | 03 | 99 | 86 | 27 |

## Brian Cain Peak Performance, LLC

www.BrianCain.com
www.BrianCainInnerCircle.com
www.ToiletsBricksFishHooksAndPride.com
www.SoWhatNextPitch.com
www.MentalConditioningManual.com

| | | | | | | | | | |
|---|---|---|---|---|---|---|---|---|---|
| 39 | 48 | 59 | 28 | 71 | 26 | 34 | 70 | 95 | 06 |
| 21 | 91 | 42 | 12 | 30 | 84 | 76 | 97 | 61 | 75 |
| 58 | 08 | 85 | 32 | 45 | 66 | 36 | 63 | 23 | 29 |
| 96 | 80 | 00 | 88 | 89 | 11 | 25 | 57 | 02 | 90 |
| 74 | 33 | 56 | 93 | 52 | 73 | 04 | 10 | 49 | 19 |
| 87 | 09 | 16 | 81 | 69 | 38 | 64 | 50 | 83 | 41 |
| 31 | 01 | 40 | 47 | 18 | 77 | 24 | 14 | 13 | 60 |
| 79 | 72 | 05 | 51 | 82 | 55 | 15 | 17 | 44 | 94 |
| 54 | 35 | 53 | 68 | 65 | 20 | 03 | 99 | 86 | 27 |
| 67 | 46 | 07 | 78 | 22 | 92 | 37 | 62 | 98 | 43 |

## Brian Cain Peak Performance, LLC

www.BrianCain.com
www.BrianCainInnerCircle.com
www.ToiletsBricksFishHooksAndPride.com
www.SoWhatNextPitch.com
www.MentalConditioningManual.com

| | | | | | | | | | |
|---|---|---|---|---|---|---|---|---|---|
| 39 | 48 | 59 | 28 | 71 | 26 | 34 | 70 | 95 | 06 |
| 21 | 91 | 42 | 12 | 30 | 84 | 76 | 97 | 61 | 75 |
| 58 | 08 | 85 | 32 | 45 | 66 | 36 | 63 | 23 | 29 |
| 96 | 80 | 00 | 88 | 89 | 11 | 25 | 57 | 02 | 90 |
| 74 | 33 | 56 | 93 | 52 | 73 | 04 | 10 | 49 | 19 |
| 87 | 09 | 16 | 81 | 69 | 38 | 64 | 50 | 83 | 41 |
| 31 | 01 | 40 | 47 | 18 | 77 | 24 | 14 | 13 | 60 |
| 79 | 72 | 05 | 51 | 82 | 55 | 15 | 17 | 44 | 94 |
| 54 | 35 | 53 | 68 | 65 | 20 | 03 | 99 | 86 | 27 |

## Brian Cain Peak Performance, LLC

www.BrianCain.com
www.BrianCainInnerCircle.com
www.ToiletsBricksFishHooksAndPride.com
www.SoWhatNextPitch.com
www.MentalConditioningManual.com

| | | | | | | | | | |
|---|---|---|---|---|---|---|---|---|---|
| 39 | 48 | 59 | 28 | 71 | 26 | 34 | 70 | 95 | 06 |
| 21 | 91 | 42 | 12 | 30 | 84 | 76 | 97 | 61 | 75 |
| 58 | 08 | 85 | 32 | 45 | 66 | 36 | 63 | 23 | 29 |
| 96 | 80 | 00 | 88 | 89 | 11 | 25 | 57 | 02 | 90 |
| 74 | 33 | 56 | 93 | 52 | 73 | 04 | 10 | 49 | 19 |
| 87 | 09 | 16 | 81 | 69 | 38 | 64 | 50 | 83 | 41 |
| 31 | 01 | 40 | 47 | 18 | 77 | 24 | 14 | 13 | 60 |
| 79 | 72 | 05 | 51 | 82 | 55 | 15 | 17 | 44 | 94 |
| 54 | 35 | 53 | 68 | 65 | 20 | 03 | 99 | 86 | 27 |
| 67 | 46 | 07 | 78 | 22 | 92 | 37 | 62 | 98 | 43 |

## Brian Cain Peak Performance, LLC

www.BrianCain.com
www.BrianCainInnerCircle.com
www.ToiletsBricksFishHooksAndPride.com
www.SoWhatNextPitch.com
www.MentalConditioningManual.com

| | | | | | | | | | |
|---|---|---|---|---|---|---|---|---|---|
| 39 | 48 | 59 | 28 | 71 | 26 | 34 | 70 | 95 | 06 |
| 21 | 91 | 42 | 12 | 30 | 84 | 76 | 97 | 61 | 75 |
| 58 | 08 | 85 | 32 | 45 | 66 | 36 | 63 | 23 | 29 |
| 96 | 80 | 00 | 88 | 89 | 11 | 25 | 57 | 02 | 90 |
| 74 | 33 | 56 | 93 | 52 | 73 | 04 | 10 | 49 | 19 |
| 87 | 09 | 16 | 81 | 69 | 38 | 64 | 50 | 83 | 41 |
| 31 | 01 | 40 | 47 | 18 | 77 | 24 | 14 | 13 | 60 |
| 79 | 72 | 05 | 51 | 82 | 55 | 15 | 17 | 44 | 94 |
| 54 | 35 | 53 | 68 | 65 | 20 | 03 | 99 | 86 | 27 |

## Brian Cain Peak Performance, LLC

www.BrianCain.com
www.BrianCainInnerCircle.com
www.ToiletsBricksFishHooksAndPride.com
www.SoWhatNextPitch.com
www.MentalConditioningManual.com

| 39 | 48 | 59 | 28 | 71 | 26 | 34 | 70 | 95 | 06 |
|----|----|----|----|----|----|----|----|----|----|
| 21 | 91 | 42 | 12 | 30 | 84 | 76 | 97 | 61 | 75 |
| 58 | 08 | 85 | 32 | 45 | 66 | 36 | 63 | 23 | 29 |
| 96 | 80 | 00 | 88 | 89 | 11 | 25 | 57 | 02 | 90 |
| 74 | 33 | 56 | 93 | 52 | 73 | 04 | 10 | 49 | 19 |
| 87 | 09 | 16 | 81 | 69 | 38 | 64 | 50 | 83 | 41 |
| 31 | 01 | 40 | 47 | 18 | 77 | 24 | 14 | 13 | 60 |
| 79 | 72 | 05 | 51 | 82 | 55 | 15 | 17 | 44 | 94 |
| 54 | 35 | 53 | 68 | 65 | 20 | 03 | 99 | 86 | 27 |
| 67 | 46 | 07 | 78 | 22 | 92 | 37 | 62 | 98 | 43 |

## Brian Cain Peak Performance, LLC

www.BrianCain.com
www.BrianCainInnerCircle.com
www.ToiletsBricksFishHooksAndPride.com
www.SoWhatNextPitch.com
www.MentalConditioningManual.com

| 39 | 48 | 59 | 28 | 71 | 26 | 34 | 70 | 95 | 06 |
|----|----|----|----|----|----|----|----|----|----|
| 21 | 91 | 42 | 12 | 30 | 84 | 76 | 97 | 61 | 75 |
| 58 | 08 | 85 | 32 | 45 | 66 | 36 | 63 | 23 | 29 |
| 96 | 80 | 00 | 88 | 89 | 11 | 25 | 57 | 02 | 90 |
| 74 | 33 | 56 | 93 | 52 | 73 | 04 | 10 | 49 | 19 |
| 87 | 09 | 16 | 81 | 69 | 38 | 64 | 50 | 83 | 41 |
| 31 | 01 | 40 | 47 | 18 | 77 | 24 | 14 | 13 | 60 |
| 79 | 72 | 05 | 51 | 82 | 55 | 15 | 17 | 44 | 94 |
| 54 | 35 | 53 | 68 | 65 | 20 | 03 | 99 | 86 | 27 |

## Brian Cain Peak Performance, LLC

www.BrianCain.com
www.BrianCainInnerCircle.com
www.ToiletsBricksFishHooksAndPride.com
www.SoWhatNextPitch.com
www.MentalConditioningManual.com

| 39 | 48 | 59 | 28 | 71 | 26 | 34 | 70 | 95 | 06 |
|----|----|----|----|----|----|----|----|----|----|
| 21 | 91 | 42 | 12 | 30 | 84 | 76 | 97 | 61 | 75 |
| 58 | 08 | 85 | 32 | 45 | 66 | 36 | 63 | 23 | 29 |
| 96 | 80 | 00 | 88 | 89 | 11 | 25 | 57 | 02 | 90 |
| 74 | 33 | 56 | 93 | 52 | 73 | 04 | 10 | 49 | 19 |
| 87 | 09 | 16 | 81 | 69 | 38 | 64 | 50 | 83 | 41 |
| 31 | 01 | 40 | 47 | 18 | 77 | 24 | 14 | 13 | 60 |
| 79 | 72 | 05 | 51 | 82 | 55 | 15 | 17 | 44 | 94 |
| 54 | 35 | 53 | 68 | 65 | 20 | 03 | 99 | 86 | 27 |
| 67 | 46 | 07 | 78 | 22 | 92 | 37 | 62 | 98 | 43 |

## Brian Cain Peak Performance, LLC

www.BrianCain.com
www.BrianCainInnerCircle.com
www.ToiletsBricksFishHooksAndPride.com
www.SoWhatNextPitch.com
www.MentalConditioningManual.com

| 39 | 48 | 59 | 28 | 71 | 26 | 34 | 70 | 95 | 06 |
|----|----|----|----|----|----|----|----|----|----|
| 21 | 91 | 42 | 12 | 30 | 84 | 76 | 97 | 61 | 75 |
| 58 | 08 | 85 | 32 | 45 | 66 | 36 | 63 | 23 | 29 |
| 96 | 80 | 00 | 88 | 89 | 11 | 25 | 57 | 02 | 90 |
| 74 | 33 | 56 | 93 | 52 | 73 | 04 | 10 | 49 | 19 |
| 87 | 09 | 16 | 81 | 69 | 38 | 64 | 50 | 83 | 41 |
| 31 | 01 | 40 | 47 | 18 | 77 | 24 | 14 | 13 | 60 |
| 79 | 72 | 05 | 51 | 82 | 55 | 15 | 17 | 44 | 94 |
| 54 | 35 | 53 | 68 | 65 | 20 | 03 | 99 | 86 | 27 |

## Brian Cain Peak Performance, LLC

www.BrianCain.com
www.BrianCainInnerCircle.com
www.ToiletsBricksFishHooksAndPride.com
www.SoWhatNextPitch.com
www.MentalConditioningManual.com

| 39 | 48 | 59 | 28 | 71 | 26 | 34 | 70 | 95 | 06 |
|----|----|----|----|----|----|----|----|----|----|
| 21 | 91 | 42 | 12 | 30 | 84 | 76 | 97 | 61 | 75 |
| 58 | 08 | 85 | 32 | 45 | 66 | 36 | 63 | 23 | 29 |
| 96 | 80 | 00 | 88 | 89 | 11 | 25 | 57 | 02 | 90 |
| 74 | 33 | 56 | 93 | 52 | 73 | 04 | 10 | 49 | 19 |
| 87 | 09 | 16 | 81 | 69 | 38 | 64 | 50 | 83 | 41 |
| 31 | 01 | 40 | 47 | 18 | 77 | 24 | 14 | 13 | 60 |
| 79 | 72 | 05 | 51 | 82 | 55 | 15 | 17 | 44 | 94 |
| 54 | 35 | 53 | 68 | 65 | 20 | 03 | 99 | 86 | 27 |
| 67 | 46 | 07 | 78 | 22 | 92 | 37 | 62 | 98 | 43 |

## Brian Cain Peak Performance, LLC

www.BrianCain.com
www.BrianCainInnerCircle.com
www.ToiletsBricksFishHooksAndPride.com
www.SoWhatNextPitch.com
www.MentalConditioningManual.com

| 39 | 48 | 59 | 28 | 71 | 26 | 34 | 70 | 95 | 06 |
|----|----|----|----|----|----|----|----|----|----|
| 21 | 91 | 42 | 12 | 30 | 84 | 76 | 97 | 61 | 75 |
| 58 | 08 | 85 | 32 | 45 | 66 | 36 | 63 | 23 | 29 |
| 96 | 80 | 00 | 88 | 89 | 11 | 25 | 57 | 02 | 90 |
| 74 | 33 | 56 | 93 | 52 | 73 | 04 | 10 | 49 | 19 |
| 87 | 09 | 16 | 81 | 69 | 38 | 64 | 50 | 83 | 41 |
| 31 | 01 | 40 | 47 | 18 | 77 | 24 | 14 | 13 | 60 |
| 79 | 72 | 05 | 51 | 82 | 55 | 15 | 17 | 44 | 94 |
| 54 | 35 | 53 | 68 | 65 | 20 | 03 | 99 | 86 | 27 |

## Brian Cain Peak Performance, LLC

www.BrianCain.com
www.BrianCainInnerCircle.com
www.ToiletsBricksFishHooksAndPride.com
www.SoWhatNextPitch.com
www.MentalConditioningManual.com

| 39 | 48 | 59 | 28 | 71 | 26 | 34 | 70 | 95 | 06 |
|----|----|----|----|----|----|----|----|----|----|
| 21 | 91 | 42 | 12 | 30 | 84 | 76 | 97 | 61 | 75 |
| 58 | 08 | 85 | 32 | 45 | 66 | 36 | 63 | 23 | 29 |
| 96 | 80 | 00 | 88 | 89 | 11 | 25 | 57 | 02 | 90 |
| 74 | 33 | 56 | 93 | 52 | 73 | 04 | 10 | 49 | 19 |
| 87 | 09 | 16 | 81 | 69 | 38 | 64 | 50 | 83 | 41 |
| 31 | 01 | 40 | 47 | 18 | 77 | 24 | 14 | 13 | 60 |
| 79 | 72 | 05 | 51 | 82 | 55 | 15 | 17 | 44 | 94 |
| 54 | 35 | 53 | 68 | 65 | 20 | 03 | 99 | 86 | 27 |
| 67 | 46 | 07 | 78 | 22 | 92 | 37 | 62 | 98 | 43 |

## Brian Cain Peak Performance, LLC

www.BrianCain.com
www.BrianCainInnerCircle.com
www.ToiletsBricksFishHooksAndPride.com
www.SoWhatNextPitch.com
www.MentalConditioningManual.com

| 39 | 48 | 59 | 28 | 71 | 26 | 34 | 70 | 95 | 06 |
|----|----|----|----|----|----|----|----|----|----|
| 21 | 91 | 42 | 12 | 30 | 84 | 76 | 97 | 61 | 75 |
| 58 | 08 | 85 | 32 | 45 | 66 | 36 | 63 | 23 | 29 |
| 96 | 80 | 00 | 88 | 89 | 11 | 25 | 57 | 02 | 90 |
| 74 | 33 | 56 | 93 | 52 | 73 | 04 | 10 | 49 | 19 |
| 87 | 09 | 16 | 81 | 69 | 38 | 64 | 50 | 83 | 41 |
| 31 | 01 | 40 | 47 | 18 | 77 | 24 | 14 | 13 | 60 |
| 79 | 72 | 05 | 51 | 82 | 55 | 15 | 17 | 44 | 94 |
| 54 | 35 | 53 | 68 | 65 | 20 | 03 | 99 | 86 | 27 |

## Brian Cain Peak Performance, LLC

www.BrianCain.com
www.BrianCainInnerCircle.com
www.ToiletsBricksFishHooksAndPride.com
www.SoWhatNextPitch.com
www.MentalConditioningManual.com

| 39 | 48 | 59 | 28 | 71 | 26 | 34 | 70 | 95 | 06 |
|----|----|----|----|----|----|----|----|----|----|
| 21 | 91 | 42 | 12 | 30 | 84 | 76 | 97 | 61 | 75 |
| 58 | 08 | 85 | 32 | 45 | 66 | 36 | 63 | 23 | 29 |
| 96 | 80 | 00 | 88 | 89 | 11 | 25 | 57 | 02 | 90 |
| 74 | 33 | 56 | 93 | 52 | 73 | 04 | 10 | 49 | 19 |
| 87 | 09 | 16 | 81 | 69 | 38 | 64 | 50 | 83 | 41 |
| 31 | 01 | 40 | 47 | 18 | 77 | 24 | 14 | 13 | 60 |
| 79 | 72 | 05 | 51 | 82 | 55 | 15 | 17 | 44 | 94 |
| 54 | 35 | 53 | 68 | 65 | 20 | 03 | 99 | 86 | 27 |
| 67 | 46 | 07 | 78 | 22 | 92 | 37 | 62 | 98 | 43 |

## Brian Cain Peak Performance, LLC

www.BrianCain.com
www.BrianCainInnerCircle.com
www.ToiletsBricksFishHooksAndPride.com
www.SoWhatNextPitch.com
www.MentalConditioningManual.com

| 39 | 48 | 59 | 28 | 71 | 26 | 34 | 70 | 95 | 06 |
|----|----|----|----|----|----|----|----|----|----|
| 21 | 91 | 42 | 12 | 30 | 84 | 76 | 97 | 61 | 75 |
| 58 | 08 | 85 | 32 | 45 | 66 | 36 | 63 | 23 | 29 |
| 96 | 80 | 00 | 88 | 89 | 11 | 25 | 57 | 02 | 90 |
| 74 | 33 | 56 | 93 | 52 | 73 | 04 | 10 | 49 | 19 |
| 87 | 09 | 16 | 81 | 69 | 38 | 64 | 50 | 83 | 41 |
| 31 | 01 | 40 | 47 | 18 | 77 | 24 | 14 | 13 | 60 |
| 79 | 72 | 05 | 51 | 82 | 55 | 15 | 17 | 44 | 94 |
| 54 | 35 | 53 | 68 | 65 | 20 | 03 | 99 | 86 | 27 |

## Brian Cain Peak Performance, LLC

www.BrianCain.com
www.BrianCainInnerCircle.com
www.ToiletsBricksFishHooksAndPride.com
www.SoWhatNextPitch.com
www.MentalConditioningManual.com

| 39 | 48 | 59 | 28 | 71 | 26 | 34 | 70 | 95 | 06 |
|----|----|----|----|----|----|----|----|----|----|
| 21 | 91 | 42 | 12 | 30 | 84 | 76 | 97 | 61 | 75 |
| 58 | 08 | 85 | 32 | 45 | 66 | 36 | 63 | 23 | 29 |
| 96 | 80 | 00 | 88 | 89 | 11 | 25 | 57 | 02 | 90 |
| 74 | 33 | 56 | 93 | 52 | 73 | 04 | 10 | 49 | 19 |
| 87 | 09 | 16 | 81 | 69 | 38 | 64 | 50 | 83 | 41 |
| 31 | 01 | 40 | 47 | 18 | 77 | 24 | 14 | 13 | 60 |
| 79 | 72 | 05 | 51 | 82 | 55 | 15 | 17 | 44 | 94 |
| 54 | 35 | 53 | 68 | 65 | 20 | 03 | 99 | 86 | 27 |
| 67 | 46 | 07 | 78 | 22 | 92 | 37 | 62 | 98 | 43 |

## Brian Cain Peak Performance, LLC

www.BrianCain.com
www.BrianCainInnerCircle.com
www.ToiletsBricksFishHooksAndPride.com
www.SoWhatNextPitch.com
www.MentalConditioningManual.com

| 39 | 48 | 59 | 28 | 71 | 26 | 34 | 70 | 95 | 06 |
|----|----|----|----|----|----|----|----|----|----|
| 21 | 91 | 42 | 12 | 30 | 84 | 76 | 97 | 61 | 75 |
| 58 | 08 | 85 | 32 | 45 | 66 | 36 | 63 | 23 | 29 |
| 96 | 80 | 00 | 88 | 89 | 11 | 25 | 57 | 02 | 90 |
| 74 | 33 | 56 | 93 | 52 | 73 | 04 | 10 | 49 | 19 |
| 87 | 09 | 16 | 81 | 69 | 38 | 64 | 50 | 83 | 41 |
| 31 | 01 | 40 | 47 | 18 | 77 | 24 | 14 | 13 | 60 |
| 79 | 72 | 05 | 51 | 82 | 55 | 15 | 17 | 44 | 94 |
| 54 | 35 | 53 | 68 | 65 | 20 | 03 | 99 | 86 | 27 |

## Brian Cain Peak Performance, LLC

www.BrianCain.com
www.BrianCainInnerCircle.com
www.ToiletsBricksFishHooksAndPride.com
www.SoWhatNextPitch.com
www.MentalConditioningManual.com

| | | | | | | | | | |
|---|---|---|---|---|---|---|---|---|---|
| 39 | 48 | 59 | 28 | 71 | 26 | 34 | 70 | 95 | 06 |
| 21 | 91 | 42 | 12 | 30 | 84 | 76 | 97 | 61 | 75 |
| 58 | 08 | 85 | 32 | 45 | 66 | 36 | 63 | 23 | 29 |
| 96 | 80 | 00 | 88 | 89 | 11 | 25 | 57 | 02 | 90 |
| 74 | 33 | 56 | 93 | 52 | 73 | 04 | 10 | 49 | 19 |
| 87 | 09 | 16 | 81 | 69 | 38 | 64 | 50 | 83 | 41 |
| 31 | 01 | 40 | 47 | 18 | 77 | 24 | 14 | 13 | 60 |
| 79 | 72 | 05 | 51 | 82 | 55 | 15 | 17 | 44 | 94 |
| 54 | 35 | 53 | 68 | 65 | 20 | 03 | 99 | 86 | 27 |
| 67 | 46 | 07 | 78 | 22 | 92 | 37 | 62 | 98 | 43 |

## Brian Cain Peak Performance, LLC

www.BrianCain.com
www.BrianCainInnerCircle.com
www.ToiletsBricksFishHooksAndPride.com
www.SoWhatNextPitch.com
www.MentalConditioningManual.com

| | | | | | | | | | |
|---|---|---|---|---|---|---|---|---|---|
| 39 | 48 | 59 | 28 | 71 | 26 | 34 | 70 | 95 | 06 |
| 21 | 91 | 42 | 12 | 30 | 84 | 76 | 97 | 61 | 75 |
| 58 | 08 | 85 | 32 | 45 | 66 | 36 | 63 | 23 | 29 |
| 96 | 80 | 00 | 88 | 89 | 11 | 25 | 57 | 02 | 90 |
| 74 | 33 | 56 | 93 | 52 | 73 | 04 | 10 | 49 | 19 |
| 87 | 09 | 16 | 81 | 69 | 38 | 64 | 50 | 83 | 41 |
| 31 | 01 | 40 | 47 | 18 | 77 | 24 | 14 | 13 | 60 |
| 79 | 72 | 05 | 51 | 82 | 55 | 15 | 17 | 44 | 94 |
| 54 | 35 | 53 | 68 | 65 | 20 | 03 | 99 | 86 | 27 |

# NOTES

27100387R00126

Made in the USA
Charleston, SC
02 March 2014